Yokai GIRLS
8
Kazuki Funatsu

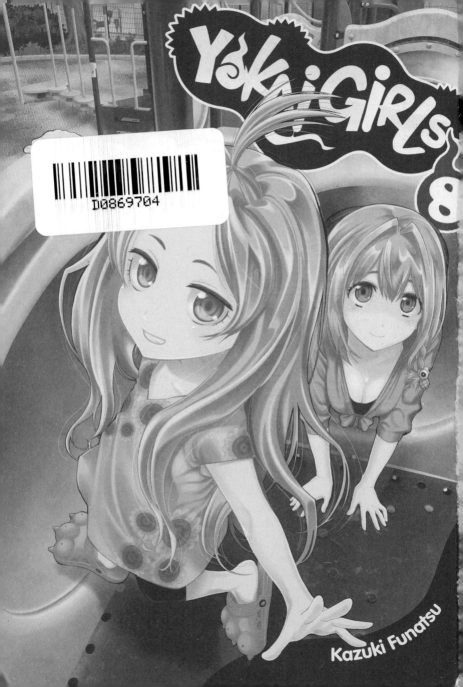

The Cast of Monster Girls!
NISHIZURU NANAO
Yatsuki's sister. She's been stuck as a spirit for the past six years, unable to return to her comatose body.
NISHIZURU YATSUKI
Works part-time in Akihabara. Can see ghosts and has gotten himself mixed up with a bunch of yokai.
AYATSUKI ROKKA
A pretty girl whom Yatsuki once helped out. Ever since, she's seemed quite taken by him. She's actually a yokai: a rokurokubi.
YOU'RE GETTING CARRIED AWAY...
KAPPER-VERT-SAN!!
CHITOSEYA MOMO
A maid who works at the maid cafe Yatsuki frequents. Her maid alias is "Moru." Prone bynature to being possessed by spirits and yokai.

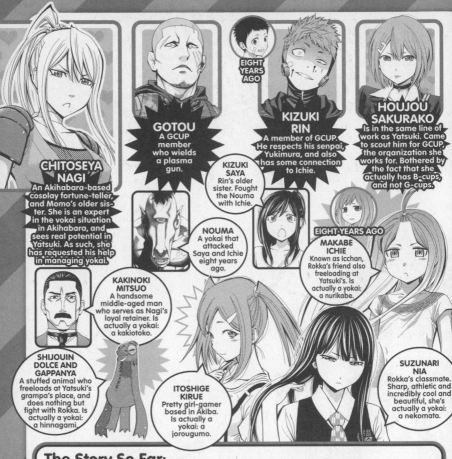

CHITOSEYA NAGI
An Akihabara-based cosplay fortune-teller, and Momo's older sister. She is an expert in the yokai situation in Akihabara, and sees real potential in Yatsuki. As such, she has requested his help in managing yokai.

GOTOU
A GCUP member who wields a plasma gun.

EIGHT YEARS AGO

KIZUKI RIN
A member of GCUP. He respects his senpai, Yukimura, and also has some connection to Ichie.

KIZUKI SAYA
Rin's older sister. Fought the Nouma with Ichie.

HOUJOU SAKURAKO
Is in the same line of work as Yatsuki. Came to scout him for GCUP, the organization she works for. Bothered by the fact that she actually has B-cups, and not G-cups.

NOUMA
A yokai that attacked Saya and Ichie eight years ago.

EIGHT-YEARS AGO
MAKABE ICHIE
Known as Icchan, Rokka's friend also freeloading at Yatsuki's. Is actually a yokai: a nurikabe.

KAKINOKI MITSUO
A handsome middle-aged man who serves as Nagi's loyal retainer. Is actually a yokai: a kakiotoko.

SHIJOUIN DOLCE AND GAPPANYA
A stuffed animal who freeloads at Yatsuki's grampa's place, and does nothing but fight with Rokka. Is actually a yokai: a hinnagami.

ITOSHIGE KIRUE
Pretty girl-gamer based in Akiba. Is actually a yokai: a jorougumo.

SUZUNARI NIA
Rokka's classmate. Sharp, athletic and incredibly cool and beautiful, she's actually a yokai: a nekomata.

The Story So Far:

Nishizuru Yatsuki is a twenty-year-old virgin working part-time at a general store in Akihabara. For some reason, he's always been able to see spirits. One day, he meets the beautiful Rokka. She's super cute, and happenstance brings them very close very fast...or it would have, but Rokka turns out to be a yokai--a rokurokubi!

Since then, a ton of yokai-related incidents have occurred in Yatsuki's life! Yatsuki has started doing yokai management in order to save his little sister, Nanao, who has been stuck as a spirit, unable to return to her body.

Doing this work has led to Yatsuki receiving an invitation to join the yokai extermination group, GCUP, and he participated in one of their missions to subdue a yokai. After that harrowing incident, Yatsuki swore to become a bridge to connect humans and yokai. Following this, Yatsuki discovers that his ghostly little sister Nanao needs ethereal energy (Shockergy) to get back to her body, so he decides to gather Shockergy. A yokai-subduing mission leads Nia and Rokka to encounter hostile GCUP forces. Meanwhile, Yatsuki and Ichie are chasing Rin, who's abducted Momo. As all this is going on, Ichie recalls her past with Rin, the young man who calls her his enemy.

YOKAI GIRLS

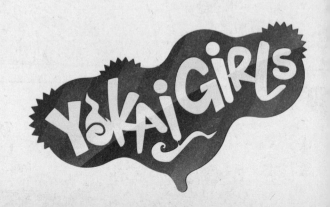

倒壁
CRASHING WALL...
NEIIIGH!!
ZU-DON
DEATH-PRESS!!!!!!
71 A Grief-Stricken Initiation...! ♪
BUH...
BUH HUH...
FOAM FOAM
FOAM
HOW DOES IT FEEL?
TO LOSE TO A YOKAI WHO CAN DO NAUGHT BUT BLOCK YOU?

FEELS RATHER ODD...
DOES IT NOT...
NOUMA?!
BWAM
71
A Grief-Stricken Initiation...! ♪

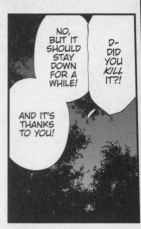

NO, BUT IT SHOULD STAY DOWN FOR A WHILE!

D-DID YOU KILL IT?!

AND IT'S THANKS TO YOU!

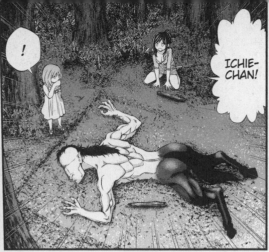

!

ICHIE-CHAN!

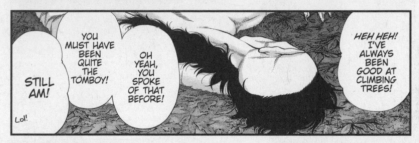

YOU MUST HAVE BEEN QUITE THE TOMBOY!

OH YEAH, YOU SPOKE OF THAT BEFORE!

STILL AM!

Lol!

HEH HEH! I'VE ALWAYS BEEN GOOD AT CLIMBING TREES!

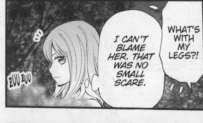

I CAN'T BLAME HER. THAT WAS NO SMALL SCARE.

WHAT'S WITH MY LEGS?!

ZUU ZUU

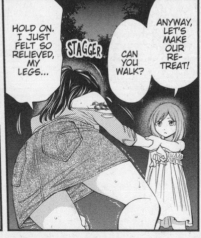

HOLD ON. I JUST FELT SO RELIEVED, MY LEGS...

STAGGER

CAN YOU WALK?

ANYWAY, LET'S MAKE OUR RETREAT!

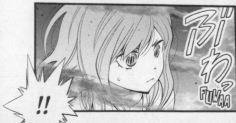

!!

FUVAA

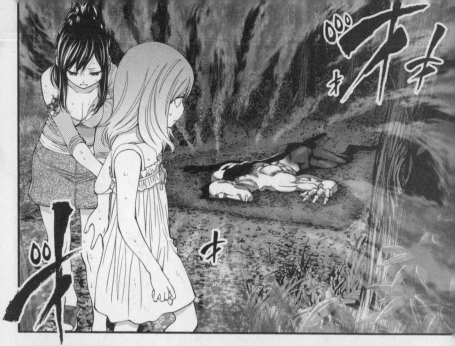

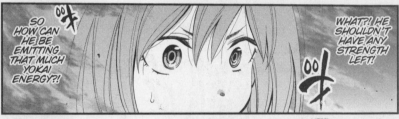

SO HOW CAN HE BE EMITTING THAT MUCH YOKAI ENERGY?!

WHAT?! HE SHOULDN'T HAVE ANY STRENGTH LEFT!

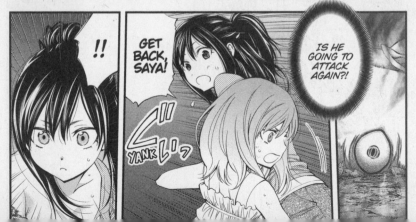

!!

GET BACK, SAYA!

IS HE GOING TO ATTACK AGAIN?!

YANK

LOOM...
WHAT IS...
BUH FUH...
FWSH
WHA?!
BEHIND US?!
ICHIE!
DASH

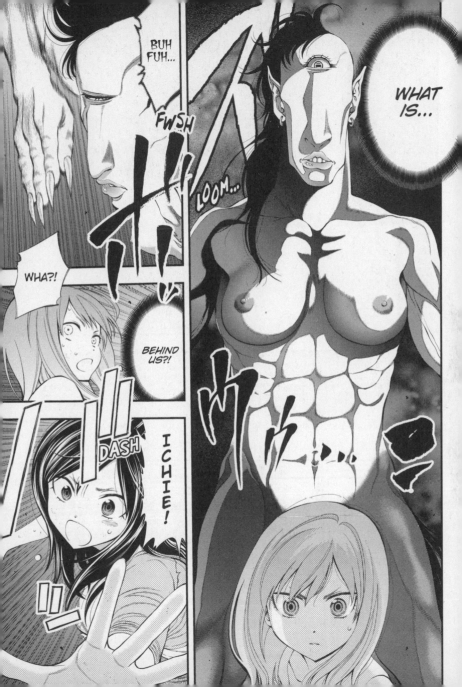

SHNK...

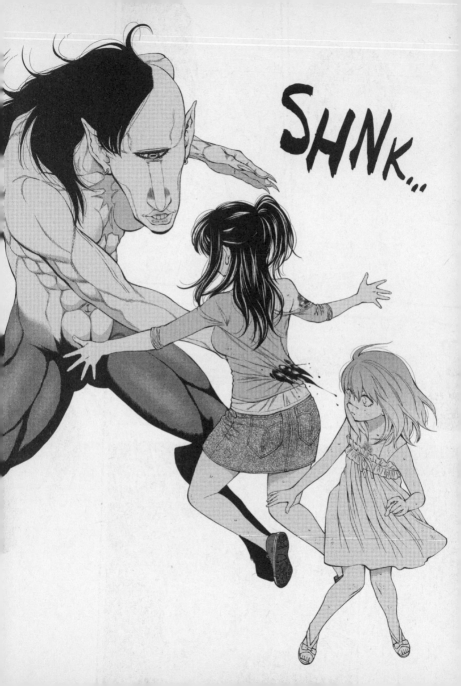

AH!
WH...
WHY...?

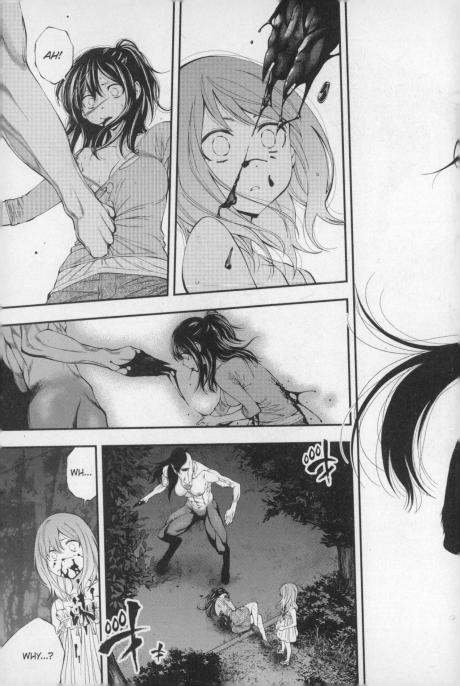

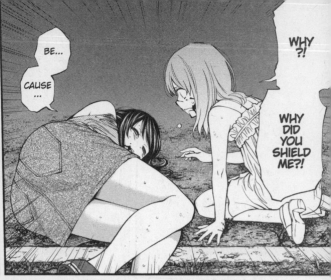

WHY ?!

BE... CAUSE...

WHY DID YOU SHIELD ME?!

THAT'S IT?! WHAT FOOLISHNESS!

YOU'RE RIN'S... GOOD FRIEND... RIGHT?

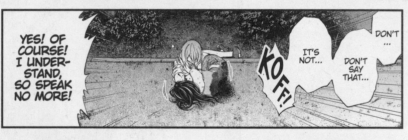

YES! OF COURSE! I UNDERSTAND, SO SPEAK NO MORE!

IT'S NOT...

DON'T SAY THAT...

DON'T...

KOFF!

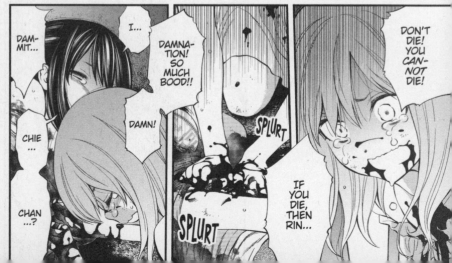

DAMMIT...

I....

DAMNATION! SO MUCH BOOD!!

DAMN!

CHIE...

CHAN...?

SPLURT

SPLURT

DON'T DIE! YOU CAN- NOT DIE!

IF YOU DIE, THEN RIN...

PLEASE...
STAY...
FRIENDS...
!...
WITH RIN...
YOU ...
CAN'T.
DON'T DIE.
PLEASE ...

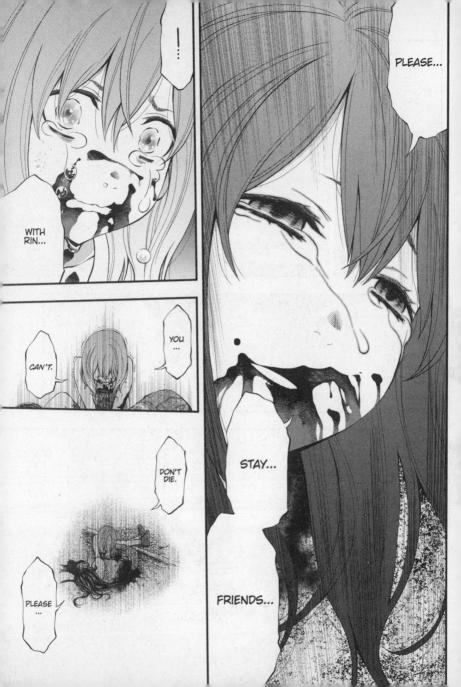

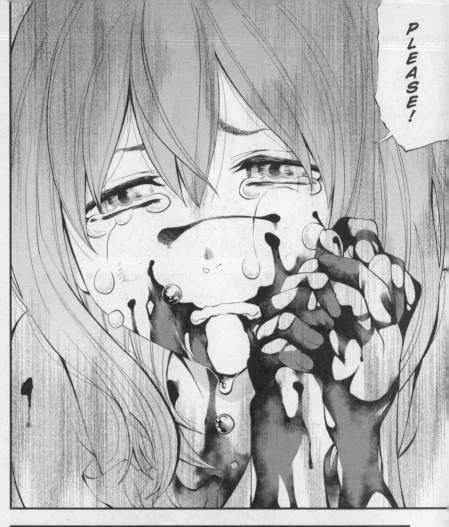

PLEASE!

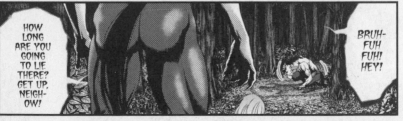

HOW LONG ARE YOU GOING TO LIE THERE? GET UP, NEIGH-OW!

BRUH-FUH FUH! HEY!

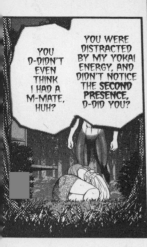

YOU D-DIDN'T EVEN THINK I HAD A M-MATE, HUH?

YOU WERE DISTRACTED BY MY YOKAI ENERGY, AND DIDN'T NOTICE THE SECOND PRESENCE, D-DID YOU?

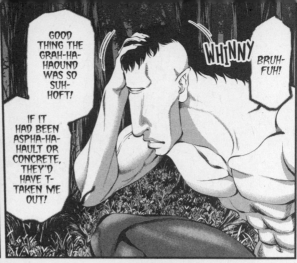

GOOD THING THE GRAH-HA-HAOUND WAS SO SUH-HOFT!

IF IT HAD BEEN ASPHA-HA-HAULT OR CONCRETE, THEY'D HAVE T-TAKEN ME OUT!

WHINNY

BRUH-FUH!

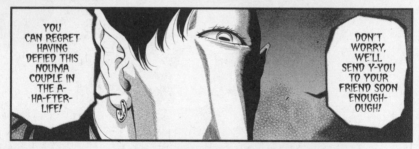

YOU CAN REGRET HAVING DEFIED THIS NOUMA COUPLE IN THE A-HA-FTER-LIFE!

DON'T WORRY, WE'LL SEND Y-YOU TO YOUR FRIEND SOON ENOUGH-OUGH!

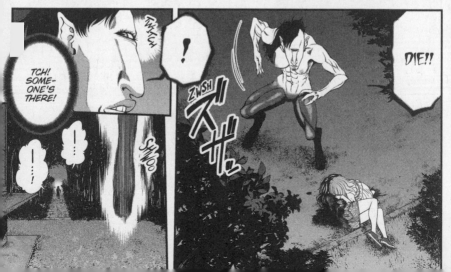

TCH! SOME-ONE'S THERE!

!

!

!

SHVOO

TATCH

ZWSH

!

DIE!!

ザッ
ZAA...
MAME...?

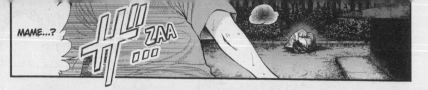

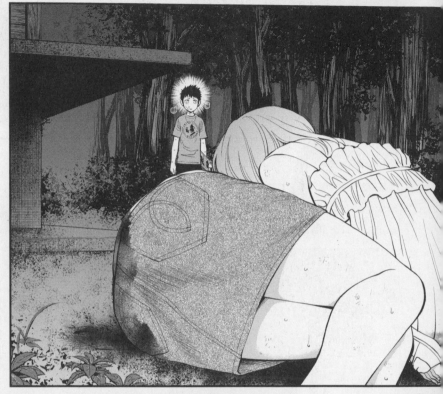

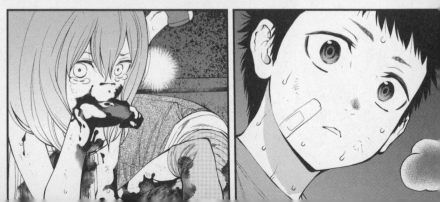

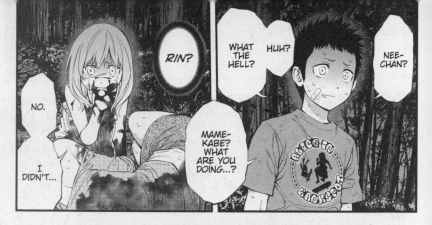

RIN?

WHAT THE HELL?

HUH?

NEE-CHAN?

NO.

I DIDN'T...

MAME-KABE? WHAT ARE YOU DOING...?

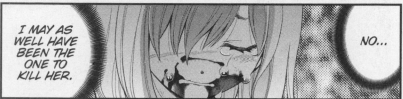

I MAY AS WELL HAVE BEEN THE ONE TO KILL HER.

NO...

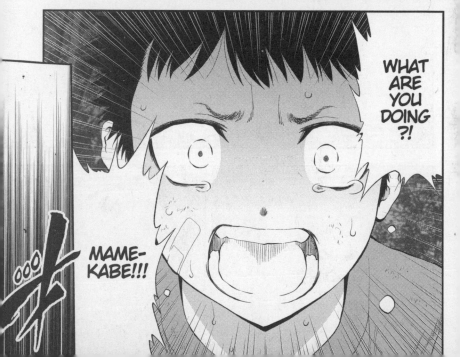

WHAT ARE YOU DOING?!

MAME-KABE!!!

OOO

THWACK

FWUMP

AH!

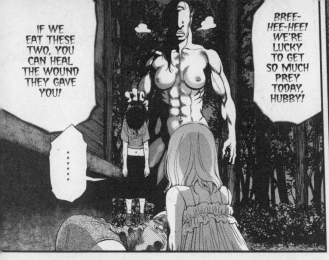

IF WE EAT THESE TWO, YOU CAN HEAL THE WOUND THEY GAVE YOU!

· · · · · ·

BREE-HEE-HEE! WE'RE LUCKY TO GET SO MUCH PREY TODAY, HUBBY!

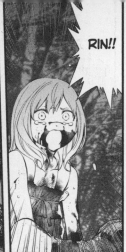

RIN!!

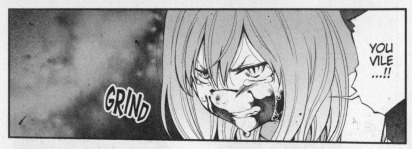

GRIND

YOU VILE ...!!

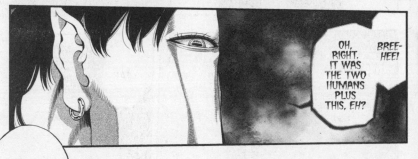

OH, RIGHT. IT WAS THE TWO HUMANS PLUS THIS, EH?

BREE-HEE!

LET GO OF THE KID!

ZAAA

ZU
ZA
ZA
ZA
ZA

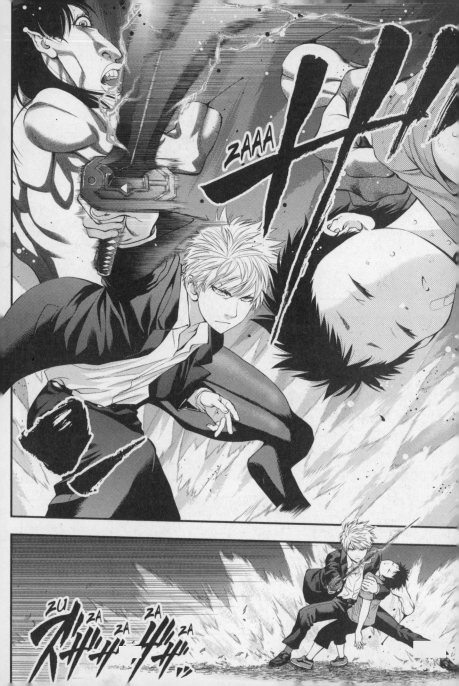

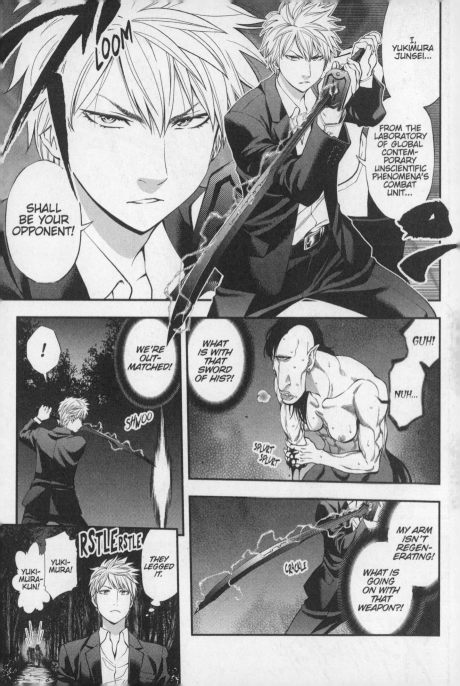

LOOM

I, YUKIMURA JUNSEI...

FROM THE LABORATORY OF GLOBAL CONTEMPORARY UNSCIENTIFIC PHENOMENA'S COMBAT UNIT...

SHALL BE YOUR OPPONENT!

!

WE'RE OUTMATCHED!

WHAT IS WITH THAT SWORD OF HIS?!

GUH!

NUH...

SHWOO

SPLURT SPLURT

MY ARM ISN'T REGENERATING!

WHAT IS GOING ON WITH THAT WEAPON?!

CRACKLE

RSTLE RSTLE

YUKIMURA-KUN!

YUKI-MURA!

THEY LEGGED IT.

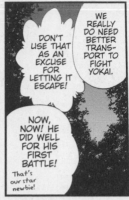

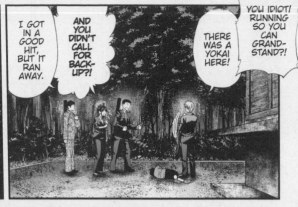

DON'T USE THAT AS AN EXCUSE FOR LETTING IT ESCAPE!

WE REALLY DO NEED BETTER TRANS-PORT TO FIGHT YOKAI.

I GOT IN A GOOD HIT, BUT IT RAN AWAY.

AND YOU DIDN'T CALL FOR BACK-UP?!

THERE WAS A YOKAI HERE!

YOU IDIOT! RUNNING SO YOU CAN GRAND-STAND?!

NOW, NOW! HE DID WELL FOR HIS FIRST BATTLE!

That's our star newbie!

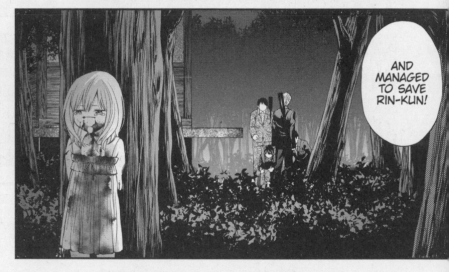

AND MANAGED TO SAVE RIN-KUN!

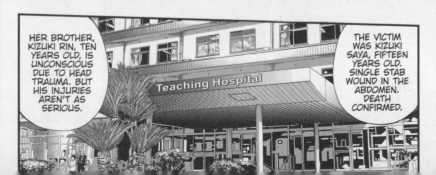

HER BROTHER, KIZUKI RIN, TEN YEARS OLD, IS UNCONSCIOUS DUE TO HEAD TRAUMA. BUT HIS INJURIES AREN'T AS SERIOUS.

Teaching Hospital

THE VICTIM WAS KIZUKI SAYA, FIFTEEN YEARS OLD. SINGLE STAB WOUND IN THE ABDOMEN. DEATH CONFIRMED.

OR SOME SORT OF TRAP TO KEEP IT FROM ESCAP- ING...

WE NEED SOME WAY TO CHASE AFTER YOKAI!

IT RAN AWAY AFTER IT SAW THAT ITS ARM DIDN'T REGENERATE.

IS THAT THE NEW PLASMA WEAPON? FANTASTIC RESULTS.

SHE WAS EATING HER...

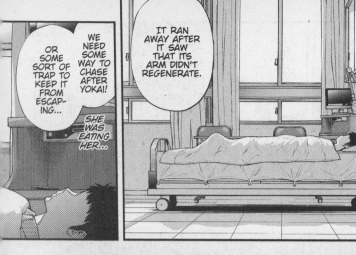

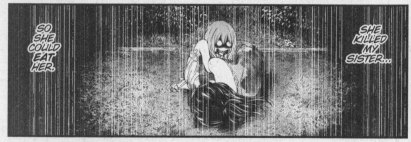

SO SHE COULD EAT HER.

SHE KILLED MY SISTER...

KILL YOKAI, RIGHT?

YOU...

HEY.

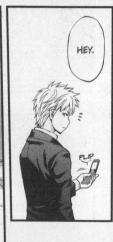

FLIP

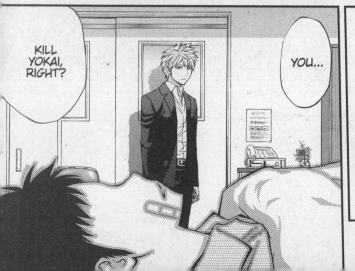

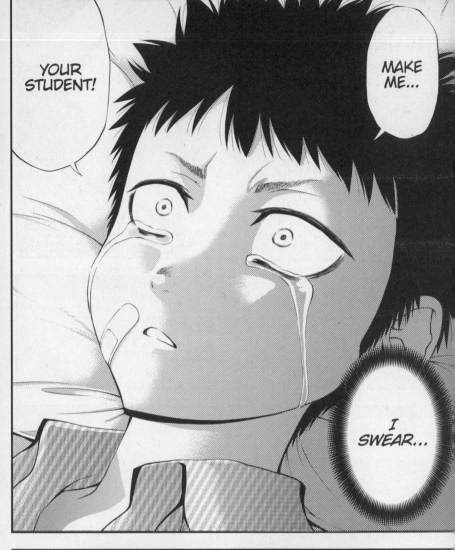

YOUR STUDENT!

MAKE ME...

I SWEAR...

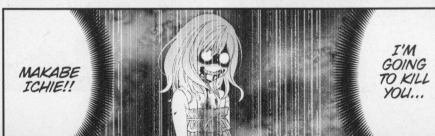

MAKABE ICHIE!!

I'M GOING TO KILL YOU...

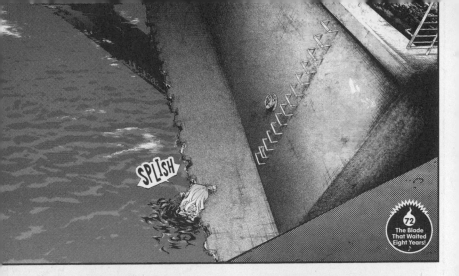

SPLISH

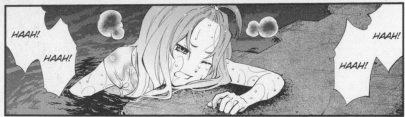

HAAH!

HAAH!

HAAH!

HAAH!

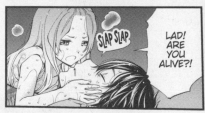

SLAP SLAP

LAD! ARE YOU ALIVE?!

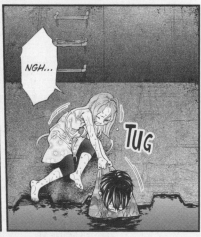

NGH...

TUG

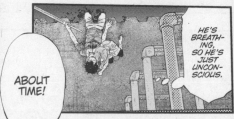

ABOUT TIME!

HE'S BREATH-ING, SO HE'S JUST UNCON-SCIOUS.

I'VE BEEN WAITING MY ASS OFF, Y'KNOW...
MAKABE ICHIE!
RIN!
72
The Blade That Waited Eight Years! ♪

WHAT'S WRONG?!
DON
YOU CAN'T BEAT ME JUST BY DODGING AROUND!
DON
DON
NGH!
THOSE ARE 20,000 DEGREE PLASMA BULLETS! IF I GET HIT WITH THAT, THERE WON'T EVEN BE DUST LEFT OF ME!
AND IT'S NEXT TO IMPOSSIBLE TO DODGE AFTER IT'S BEEN FIRED!
ALL I CAN DO IS KEEP MOVING AROUND SO THAT HE CAN'T SET HIS SIGHTS ON ME!
I GOT THIS!
BYUU
HINNA-GAMI!
JUST TRY AND CATCH ME...
THE SPEED KING, SHIJOUIN DOLCE AND GAPPAN--
ZAAA
!

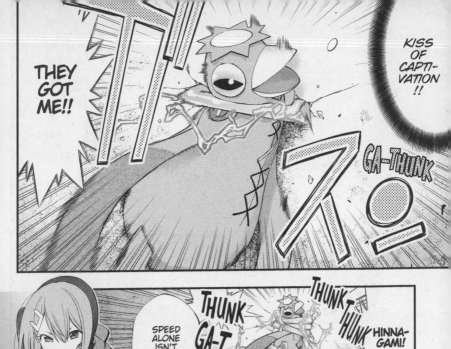

KISS OF CAPTIVATION!!

THEY GOT ME!!

GA-THUNK

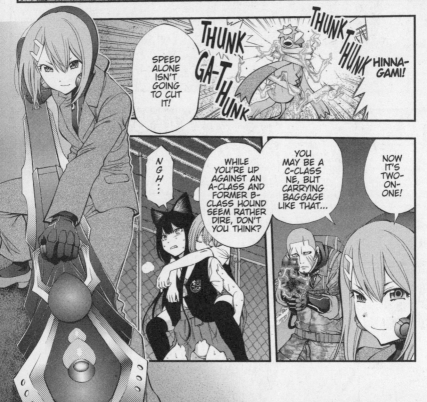

SPEED ALONE ISN'T GOING TO CUT IT!

THUNK GA-THUNK

THUNK THUNK

HINNAGAMI!

NGH...

WHILE YOU'RE UP AGAINST AN A-CLASS AND FORMER B-CLASS HOUND SEEM RATHER DIRE, DON'T YOU THINK?

YOU MAY BE A C-CLASS NE, BUT CARRYING BAGGAGE LIKE THAT...

NOW IT'S TWO-ON-ONE!

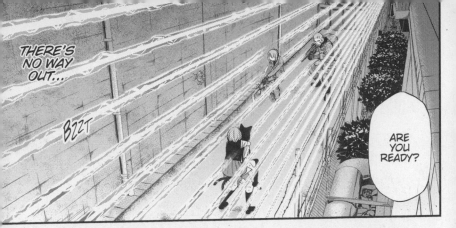

THERE'S NO WAY OUT...

BZZT

ARE YOU READY?

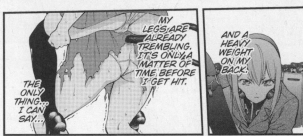

THE ONLY THING... I CAN SAY...

MY LEGS ARE ALREADY TREMBLING. IT'S ONLY A MATTER OF TIME BEFORE I GET HIT.

AND A HEAVY WEIGHT ON MY BACK...

TWO POWERFUL FIGHTERS IN FRONT OF ME...

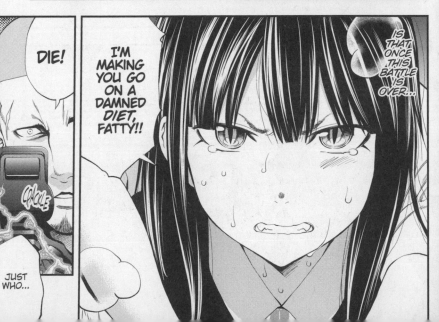

DIE!

JUST WHO...

I'M MAKING YOU GO ON A DAMNED DIET, FATTY!!

CRACKLE

IS THAT ONCE THIS BATTLE IS OVER...

ARE YOU CALL-ING A FATTY ?!
GWOO
FWUMP

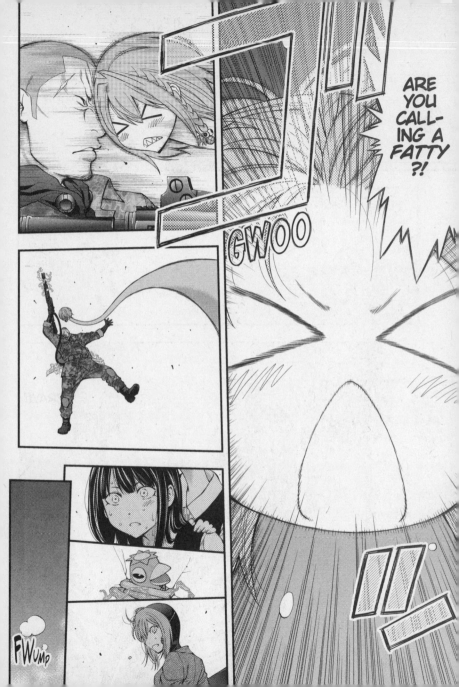

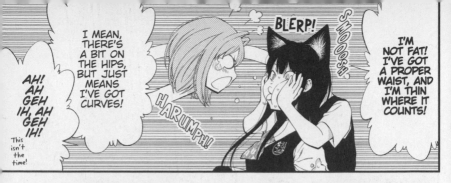

I MEAN, THERE'S A BIT ON THE HIPS, BUT JUST MEANS I'VE GOT CURVES!

AH! AH GEH IH, AH GEH IH!

This isn't the time!

BLERP!

SMOOSH!

HARUMPH!

I'M NOT FAT! I'VE GOT A PROPER WAIST, AND I'M THIN WHERE IT COUNTS!

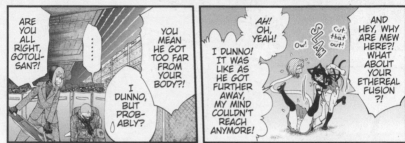

ARE YOU ALL RIGHT, GOTOU-SAN?!

· · · · ·

YOU MEAN HE GOT TOO FAR FROM YOUR BODY?!

I DUNNO, BUT PROB-ABLY?

AH! OH, YEAH!

I DUNNO! IT WAS LIKE AS HE GOT FURTHER AWAY, MY MIND COULDN'T REACH ANYMORE!

Ow!

SLAP

Cut that out!

AND HEY, WHY ARE MEW HERE?! WHAT ABOUT YOUR ETHEREAL FUSION?!

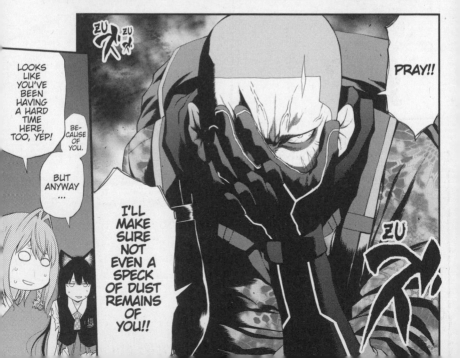

ZU ZU

LOOKS LIKE YOU'VE BEEN HAVING A HARD TIME HERE, TOO, YEP!

BE-CAUSE OF YOU.

BUT ANYWAY...

PRAY!!

I'LL MAKE SURE NOT EVEN A SPECK OF DUST REMAINS OF YOU!!

ZU

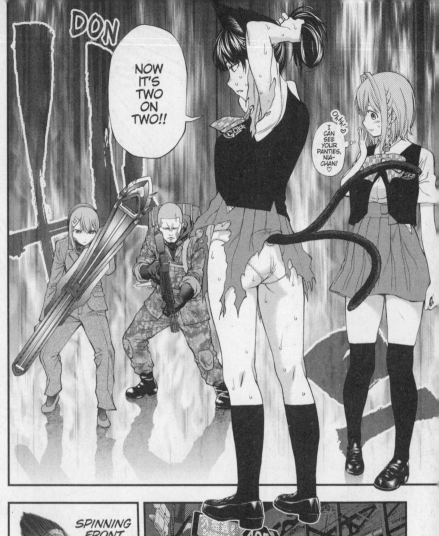

DON

NOW IT'S TWO ON TWO!!

Ohh! ♡
I CAN SEE YOUR PANTIES, NIA-CHAN! ♡

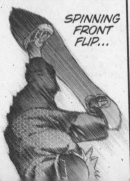

SPINNING FRONT FLIP...

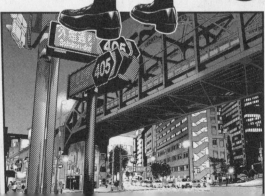

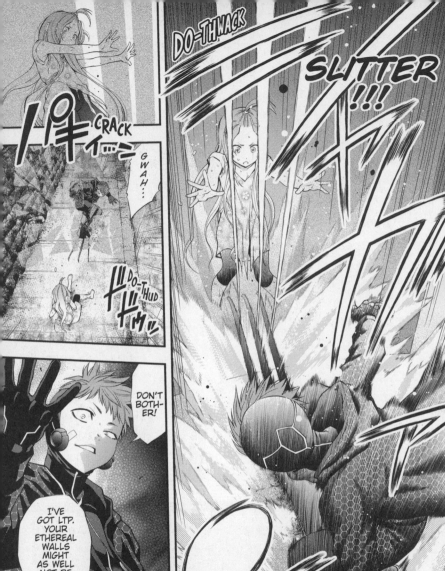

DO-THWACK

SLITTER
!!!

パキ CRACK
イ"="

GWAH...

DO-THUD

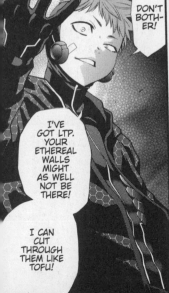

DON'T BOTHER!

I'VE GOT LTP. YOUR ETHEREAL WALLS MIGHT AS WELL NOT BE THERE!

I CAN CUT THROUGH THEM LIKE TOFU!

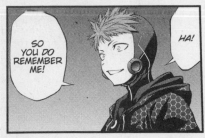

SO YOU DO REMEMBER ME!

HA!

RIN...

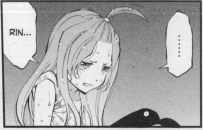

......

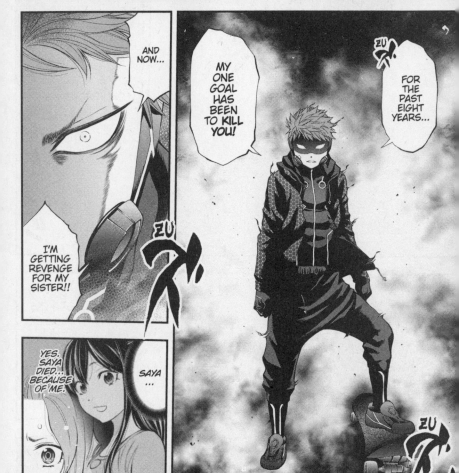

AND NOW...

MY ONE GOAL HAS BEEN TO KILL YOU!

FOR THE PAST EIGHT YEARS...

ZU

I'M GETTING REVENGE FOR MY SISTER!!

ZU

YES. SAYA DIED... BECAUSE OF ME.

SAYA...

ZU

ZU

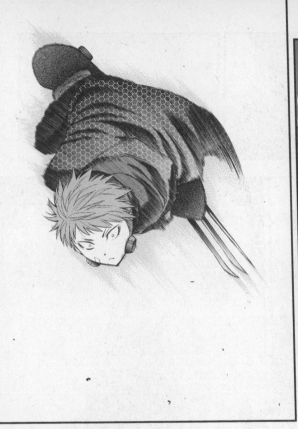
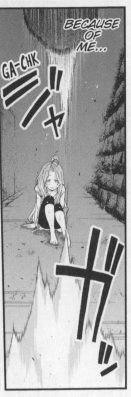

BECAUSE OF ME...

GA-CHK

GO SAY YOUR APOLOGIES TO HER ON THE OTHER SIDE!

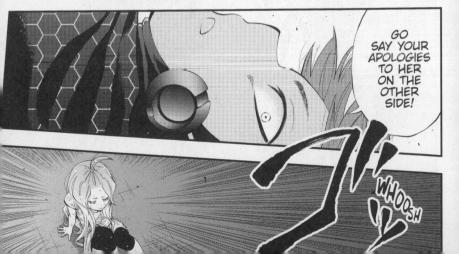

WHOOSH

ICCHAN!!!!
!!
GA-THWAM
SKIIID

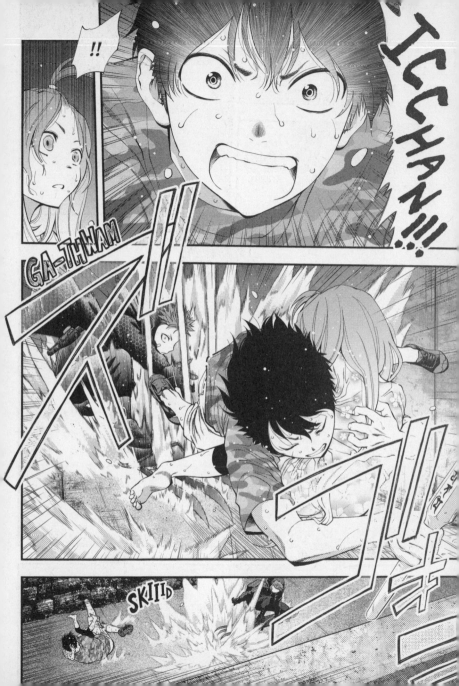

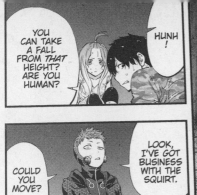

YOU CAN TAKE A FALL FROM *THAT* HEIGHT? ARE YOU HUMAN?

HUNH!

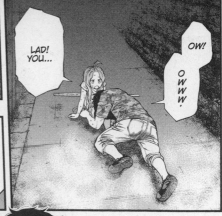

LAD! YOU...

OW! OWWW.

COULD YOU MOVE?

LOOK, I'VE GOT BUSINESS WITH THE SQUIRT.

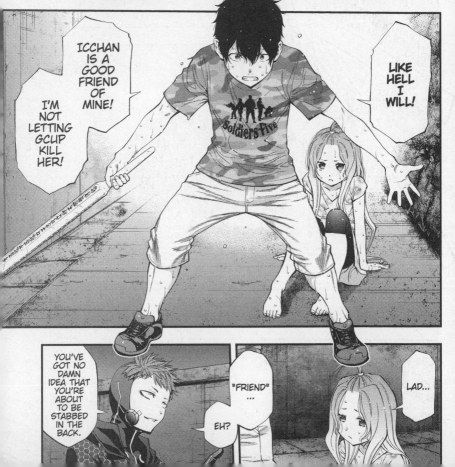

ICCHAN IS A GOOD FRIEND OF MINE!

I'M NOT LETTING GCUP KILL HER!

LIKE HELL I WILL!

YOU'VE GOT NO DAMN IDEA THAT YOU'RE ABOUT TO BE STABBED IN THE BACK.

"FRIEND"... EH?

LAD...

BUT I'M GONNA KNOCK YOUR ASS OUT, FIRST!
CLACK
HGYUUU
HYAAAAH!
DON
WHOA!
HYUUUUN
HYAA-HAAH!
YOU THINK YOU CAN TAKE ME WITH THAT WOODEN SWORD?!
THWACK
THUNK
THWACK

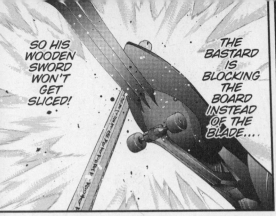

SO HIS WOODEN SWORD WON'T GET SLICED!

THE BASTARD IS BLOCKING THE BOARD INSTEAD OF THE BLADE....

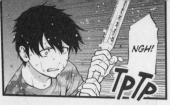

NGH!

TPTP

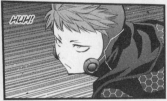

HUH!

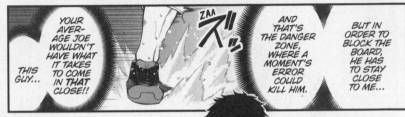

YOUR AVERAGE JOE WOULDN'T HAVE WHAT IT TAKES TO COME IN *THAT* CLOSE!!

THIS GUY...

ZAA ズッ

AND THAT'S THE DANGER ZONE, WHERE A MOMENT'S ERROR COULD KILL HIM.

BUT IN ORDER TO BLOCK THE BOARD, HE HAS TO STAY CLOSE TO ME...

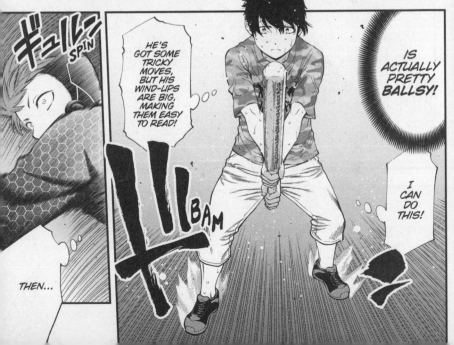

ギュルッ SPIN

HE'S GOT SOME TRICKY MOVES, BUT HIS WIND-UPS ARE BIG, MAKING THEM EASY TO READ!

IS ACTUALLY PRETTY BALLSY!

I CAN DO THIS!

BAM

THEN...

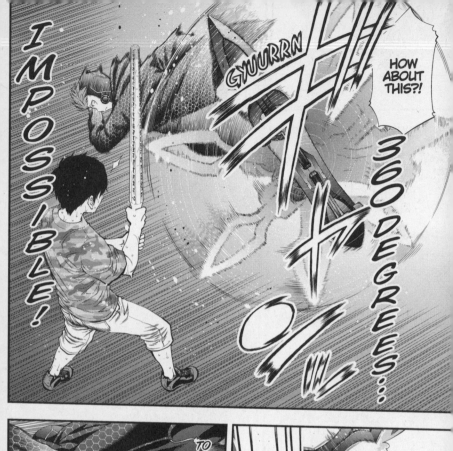

IMPOSSIBLE!

GYUURRN

HOW ABOUT THIS?!

360 DEGREES...

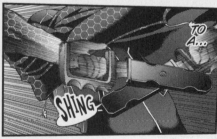

SHING

TO A...

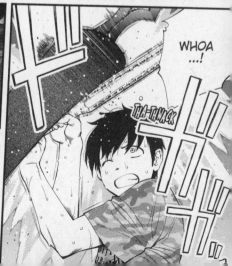

WHOA....!

THA-THWACK

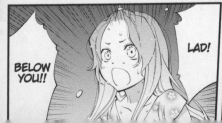

LAD!

BELOW YOU!!

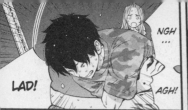

NGH...

LAD!

AGH!

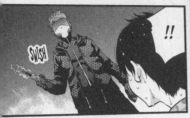

SLSH

!!

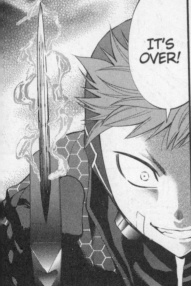

IT'S OVER!

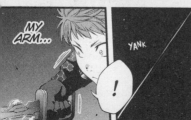

MY ARM...

YANK

!

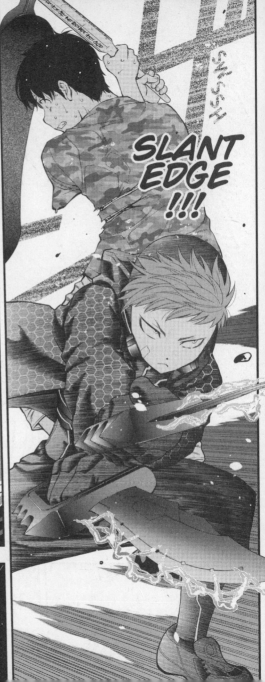

SLSSH

SLANT EDGE!!!

THREAD?!
I'M NOT LETTING YOU KILL HIM!
SORRY, BUT...
'CAUSE HE'S MY HONEY! ♡

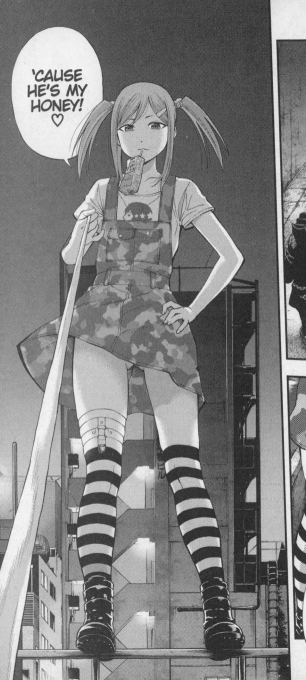

'CAUSE HE'S MY HONEY! ♡

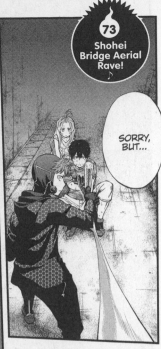

SORRY, BUT...

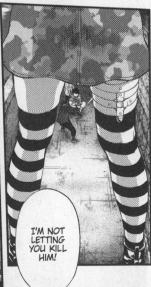

I'M NOT LETTING YOU KILL HIM!

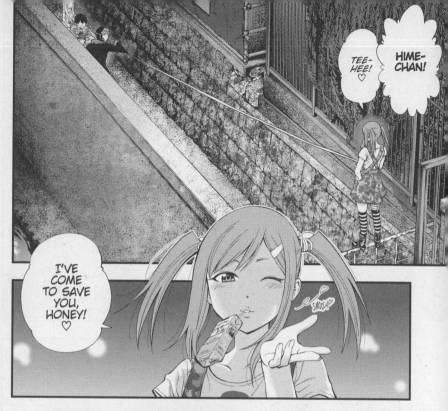

TEE-HEE! ♡

HIME-CHAN!

I'VE COME TO SAVE YOU, HONEY! ♡

SMOOCH ♡

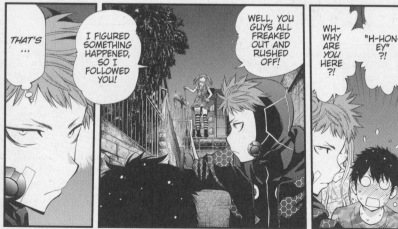

THAT'S ...

I FIGURED SOMETHING HAPPENED, SO I FOLLOWED YOU!

WELL, YOU GUYS ALL FREAKED OUT AND RUSHED OFF!

WH-WHY ARE YOU HERE?!

"H-HON-EY" ?!

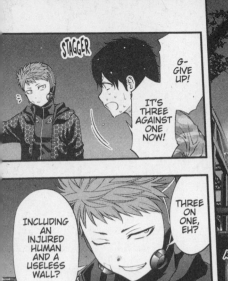

STAGGER

G-GIVE UP!

IT'S THREE AGAINST ONE NOW!

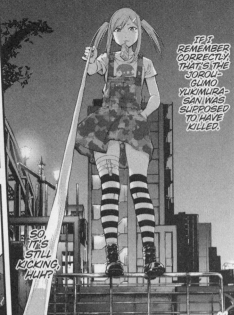

IF I REMEMBER CORRECTLY, THAT'S THE JOROU-GUMO YUKIMURA-SAN WAS SUPPOSED TO HAVE KILLED.

SO, IT'S STILL KICKING, HUH?

INCLUDING AN INJURED HUMAN AND A USELESS WALL?

THREE ON ONE, EH?

HA!

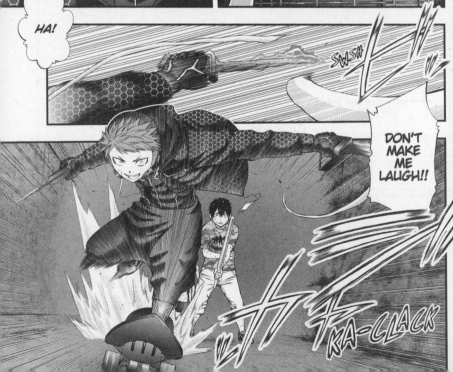

SWSH

DON'T MAKE ME LAUGH!!

KA-CLACK

GYURRN
OH?
THWAM
WHOOPS!
PTOO!
SMACK

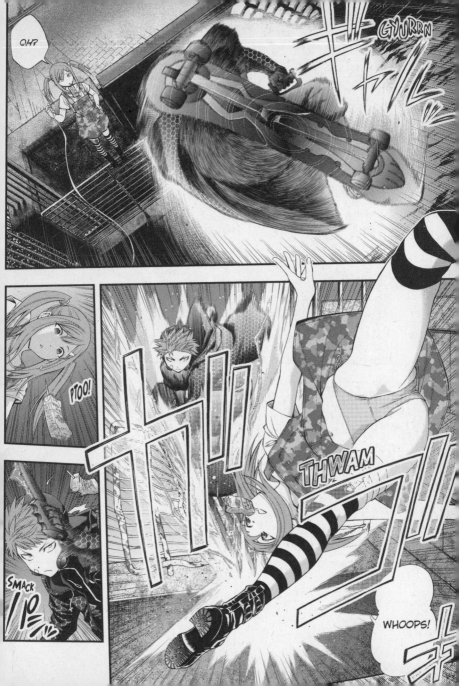

FWSH
HOP
WAY TOO SLOW!
HOP
HOP
HOP
HOP
HOP
HOP
HIME-CHAN!!
WATCH ME, HONEY! ♡
I'LL FINISH THIS WITH STYLE!

OO
OOO
SO THAT'S YOUR TRUE FORM, MONSTER!
FWSH
HEY!
ISN'T IT KINDA MEAN TO CALL A CUTE GIRL LIKE ME A MONSTER?!
THA-THWAK
WHATEVER!
THWAK
KA-THWACK
......

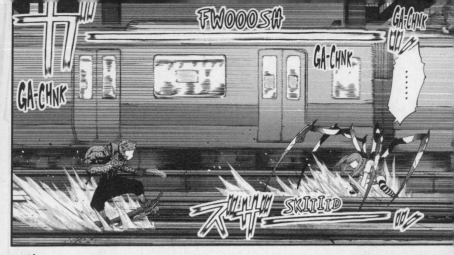

FWOOOSH

GA-CHNK

GA-CHNK

GA-CHNK

GA-CHNK

SKIIIID

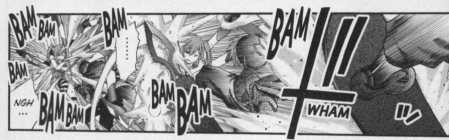

BAM BAM

BAM

BAM

BAM

NGH...

BAM BAM

BAM BAM

WHAM

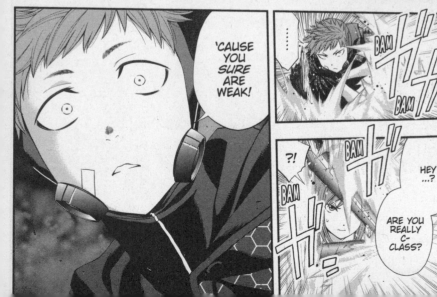

'CAUSE YOU SURE ARE WEAK!

BAM

BAM

?!

BAM

HEY...?

ARE YOU REALLY C-CLASS?

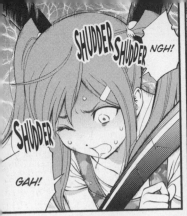

SHUDDER SHUDDER NGH!

SHUDDER

GAH!

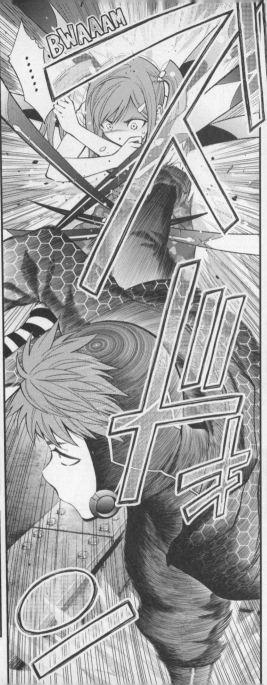

BWAAAM

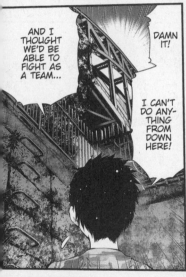

AND I THOUGHT WE'D BE ABLE TO FIGHT AS A TEAM...

DAMN IT!

I CAN'T DO ANY-THING FROM DOWN HERE!

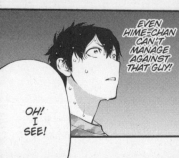

EVEN HIME-CHAN CAN'T MANAGE AGAINST THAT GUY!

OH! I SEE!

LTP DESTROYS ETHEREAL PARTICLES, SO YOU HEAL SLOW AND YOUR YOKAI POWER IS WEAKENED!

THAT'S WHERE YUKI-MURA-SAN GOT YOU, HUH?

......

BAM

BAM

BAM

RIGHT NOW, YOU'RE D-CLASS AT MOST!

......

OOZE

BAM

GUH...

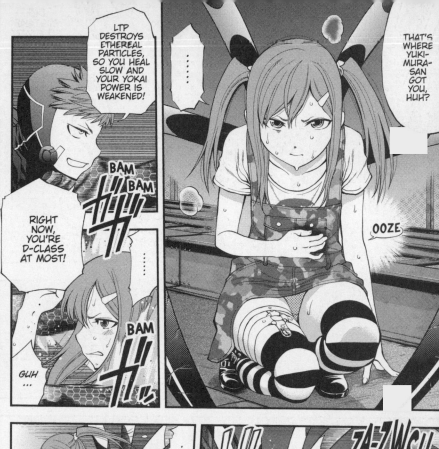

FWP

GASHAN

ZA-ZWSH

CLACK

YOU'RE JUST GONNA RUN AWAY?!

C'MON, WHAT THE HELL?

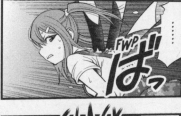

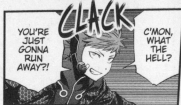

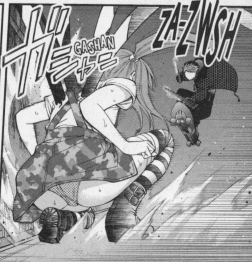

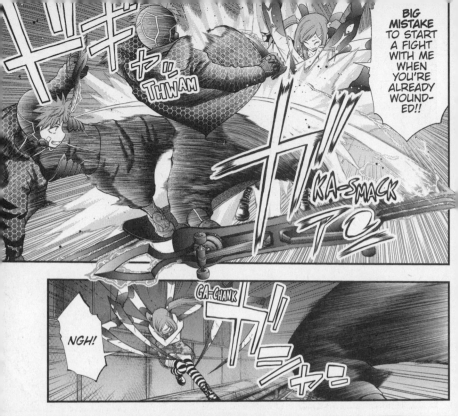

BIG MISTAKE TO START A FIGHT WITH ME WHEN YOU'RE ALREADY WOUNDED!!

ドドド

ドッ THWAM

ガ KA-SMACK

ガ GA-CHANK

NGH!

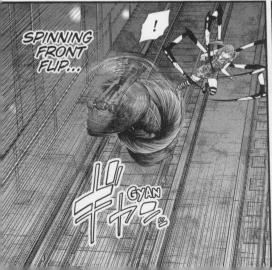

SPINNING FRONT FLIP...

!

ギャン GYAN

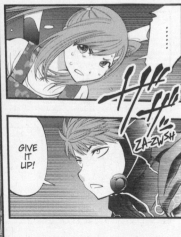

ザッ ZA-ZWSH

GIVE IT UP!

ZU-DON
SLITTER
!!!
NGH...
AAH!

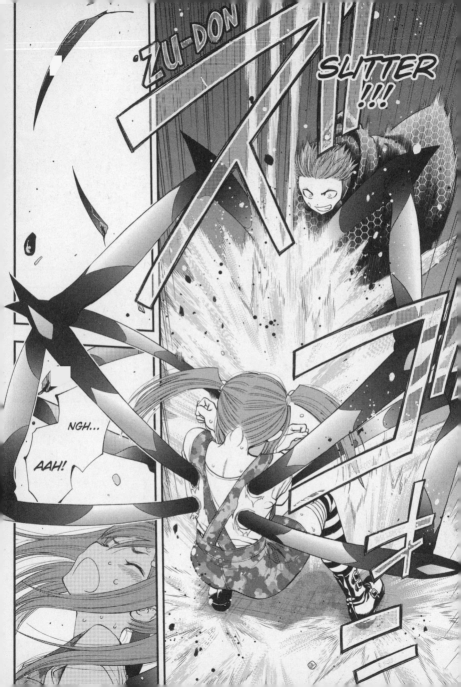

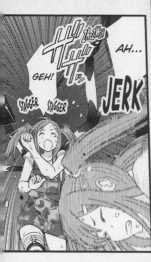

ZA-ZZSH

GEH!

HLH
HLH

STAGGER STAGGER

AH...

JERK

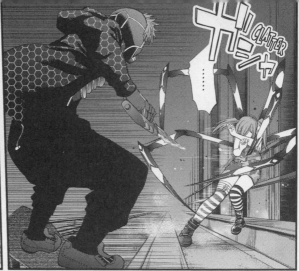

CLATTER

......

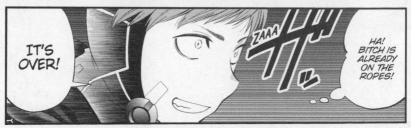

IT'S OVER!

ZAAA HLH

HA! BITCH IS ALREADY ON THE ROPES!

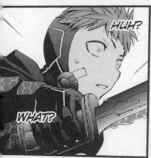

HUH?

WHAT?

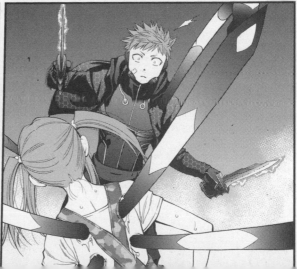

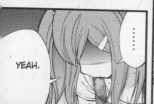

......

YEAH.

IT IS OVER!
THE THREAD?!
SHE ACTED LIKE SHE WAS RUNNING AWAY...BUT SHE WAS ACTUALLY WEAVING A WEB?!
SO THAT WEIRD STAGGERING SHE MADE, SHE WAS DUCKING UNDER THE WEB!!

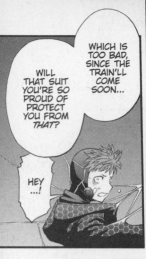

WILL THAT SUIT YOU'RE SO PROUD OF PROTECT YOU FROM *THAT*?

WHICH IS TOO BAD, SINCE THE TRAIN'LL COME SOON...

HEY ...!

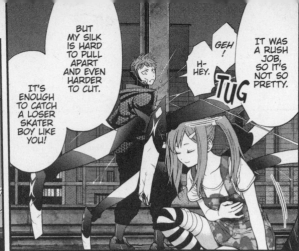

IT'S ENOUGH TO CATCH A LOSER SKATER BOY LIKE YOU!

BUT MY SILK IS HARD TO PULL APART AND EVEN HARDER TO CUT.

IT WAS A RUSH JOB, SO IT'S NOT SO PRETTY.

GEH!

H-HEY.

TUG

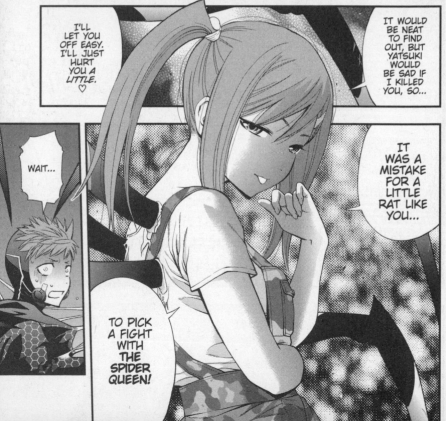

I'LL LET YOU OFF EASY. I'LL JUST HURT YOU A LITTLE. ♡

IT WOULD BE NEAT TO FIND OUT, BUT YATSUKI WOULD BE SAD IF I KILLED YOU, SO...

IT WAS A MISTAKE FOR A LITTLE RAT LIKE YOU...

WAIT...

TO PICK A FIGHT WITH **THE SPIDER QUEEN**!

GOT-CHA!
BLEAH!
!
FWEEE
ARC JET THRUST-ERS...
ACTI-VATE!!!
BWOOSH
!!
VRRRRRRR
KA-CLACK
CLACK
CLACK

HA HA!
YOU THINK YOU CAN CUT MY THREAD WITH THAT?!
GET READY TO SNAP RIGHT BACK TO ME!
TURN
I JUST HAVE TO GET TO A SPOT WHERE HE WON'T HIT ME WHEN HE COMES BACK.
BOING ⟷ BOING
Huh?
So?
I'M NOT TRYING TO BREAK IT!
FWOO
BWOOSH
CRACK
MY BEAR SUIT IS SPECIALLY MADE!
I AIN'T NO RAT!
OOO
!
ARC JET THRUSTERS...

HEDGEHOG BULLET!!!
GA-SLAAM
I'M A HEDGE-HOG!!!

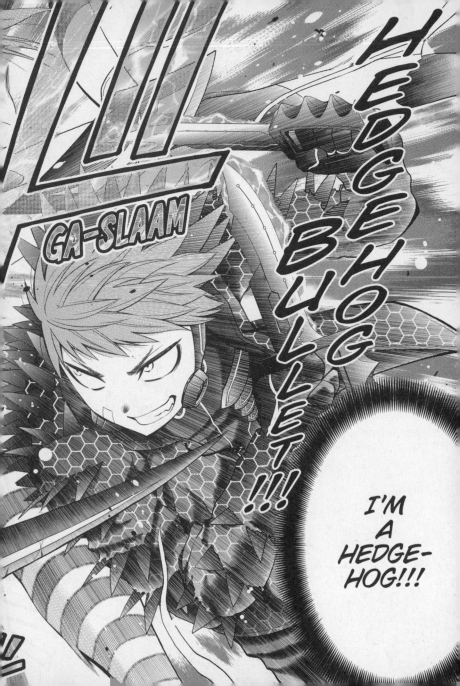

NO WAY...
YOU'VE GOT TO BE...
KIDDING ME.
THUD
CRAP!
I CAN'T EVEN SEE WHAT'S GOING ON FROM DOWN HERE!

DAMN!
WE'VE GOT NO CHOICE!
ICCHAN!
!
FUSE WITH ME!
WHAT?

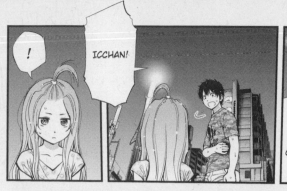

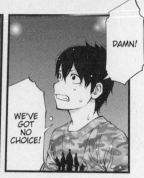

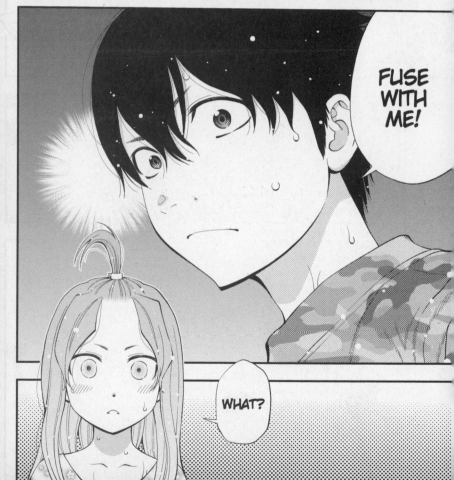

FLASH
ぱっ
TPTP
HUH? THAT GIRL...!
NAH, COULDN'T BE.
Ha ha!
I HAVE TO SAVE HER!
MOMO!
PLEASE BE SAFE!!
BUT...
FIRST ...!!

74
I Trust You...! ♪

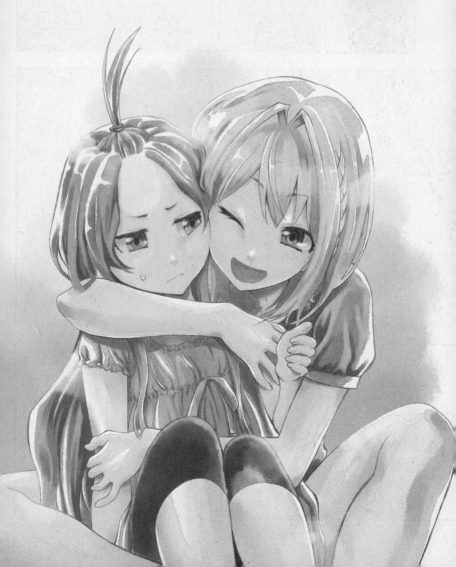

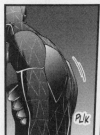

PLIK

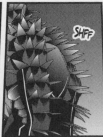

SHFF

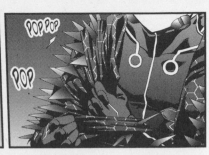

POP POP

POP

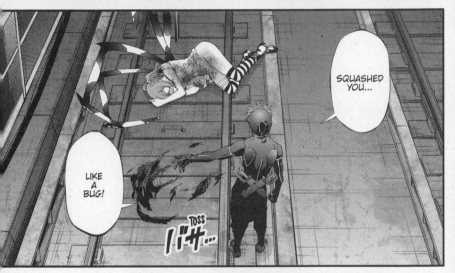

SQUASHED YOU...

LIKE A BUG!

TOSS バサ...

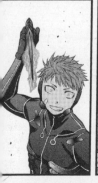

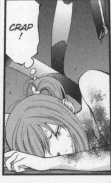

CRAP!

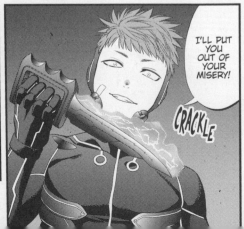

I'LL PUT YOU OUT OF YOUR MISERY!

CRACKLE

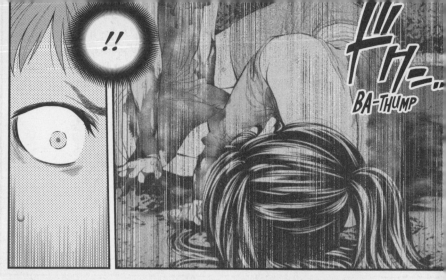

!!

ド…ッ…
BA-THUMP

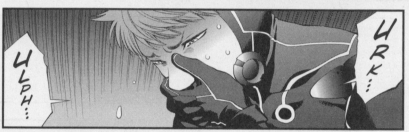

URK...

ULPH...

DAMMIT!

405
405

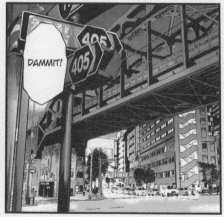

WHAT'S WITH HIM?

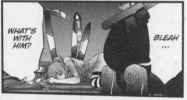

BLEAH...

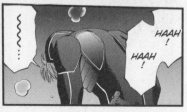

HAAH!

HAAH!

...

YOU HEARD ME!!
LET'S FUSE OUR BODIES!!
WHAT?
IT'LL BE OKAY! IF I CAN DO IT WITH ROKKA, I'M *SURE* I CAN DO IT WITH YOU, TOO!
WAIT ...
IT MIGHT BE UNCOMFORTABLE AT FIRST, BUT IT'S ACTUALLY NOT A BIG DEAL!
HEY ...
ROKKA GOT USED TO IT RIGHT AWAY, SO I'M SURE YOU WILL, TOO!
UM ...
HOLD ON!
WE *HAVE* TO DO IT IN ORDER TO SURVIVE THIS!
!
!
!

THIS WAY, ICCHAN!

OH, THEY WERE TALKING ABOUT AQUARI-ON?

VEC-TOR?

SNEAK SNEAK SNEAK

FUSING THREE VECTOR MACHINES MAKES A GIANT ROBOT!

Y-Y-Y-YEAH!

!!

YOU THINK HE'S A PERV?

Should we call the police?

HEY, DOESN'T THAT SEEM SKETCHY?!

And they're both soaking wet.

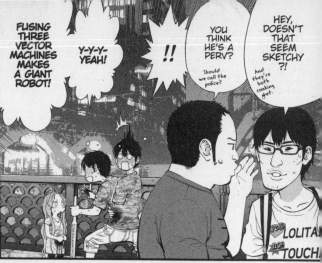

LOLITA TOUCH.

THOUGH FOR A MOMENT, I DID MISCON-STRUE HIM.

I-I KNOW!

Don't emphasize it! 'Tis embar-rassing!

NOTHING WEIRD.

J-JUST SO WE'RE CLEAR, I MEANT ETHEREAL FUSION, OKAY?!

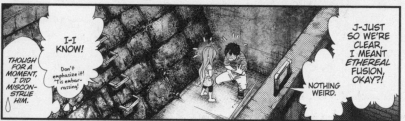

!

GET THROUGH WHAT?

YEAH! SO EVEN IF WE CAN'T BEAT HIM, AT LEAST WE'LL HAVE A SOLID DEFENSE.

A SHIELD? ME?

THINKING ABOUT HOW IT WORKED WITH ROKKA, I FIGURE MAYBE YOU'D BECOME A GIANT SHIELD!

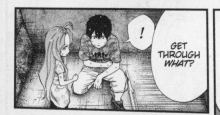

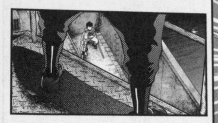

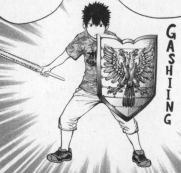

GASHIING

SO...
WE'RE BACK TO TWO-ON-ONE, EH?
URK...
WELL...
ONE OF YOU ISN'T GONNA BE ANY HELP, SO I GUESS IT'S MORE LIKE ONE-ON-ONE.
HIME-CHAN!
......
Oww!
S-SORRY.
I BLEW IT.
......
NGH!

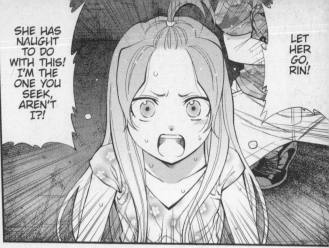

SHE HAS NAUGHT TO DO WITH THIS! I'M THE ONE YOU SEEK, AREN'T I?!

LET HER GO, RIN!

HA!

NOTHING TO DO WITH THIS?

THAT'S RIGHT!

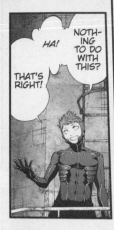

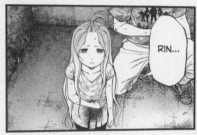

RIN...

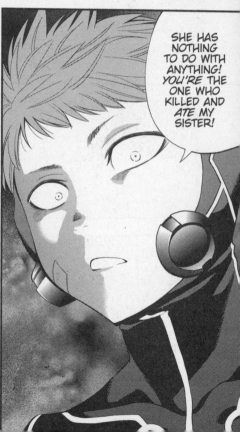

SHE HAS NOTHING TO DO WITH ANYTHING! *YOU'RE* THE ONE WHO KILLED AND *ATE* MY SISTER!

AND ATE...?

KILLED...

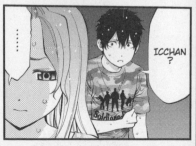

......

ICCHAN?

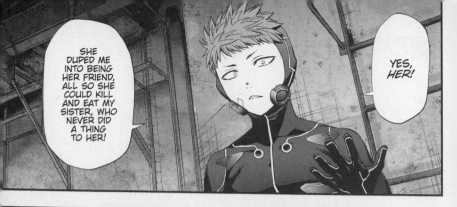

SHE DUPED ME INTO BEING HER FRIEND, ALL SO SHE COULD KILL AND EAT MY SISTER, WHO NEVER DID A THING TO HER!

YES, HER!

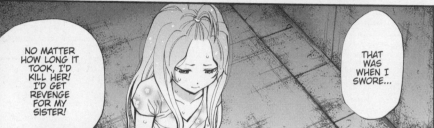

NO MATTER HOW LONG IT TOOK, I'D KILL HER! I'D GET REVENGE FOR MY SISTER!

THAT WAS WHEN I SWORE...

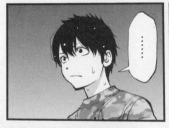

......

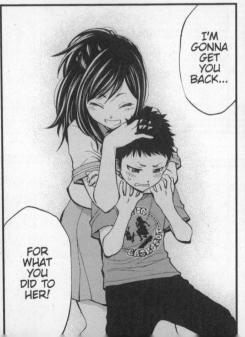

I'M GONNA GET YOU BACK...

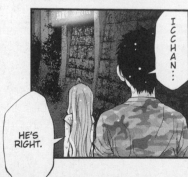

ICCHAN...

HE'S RIGHT.

FOR WHAT YOU DID TO HER!

I ESSENTIALLY DID KILL SAYA.
I...
......
WELL.
ALL RIGHT THEN.

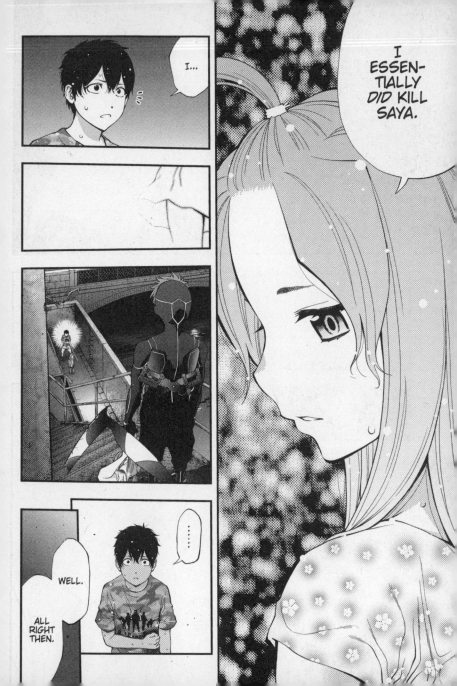

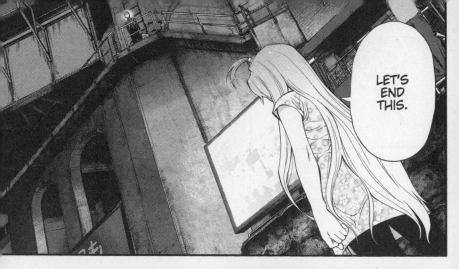

LET'S END THIS.

YOU'D COME TO TAKE MY LIFE.

THAT SOMEDAY...

I HAD AN INKLING...

ICCHA--

OW!

HA!

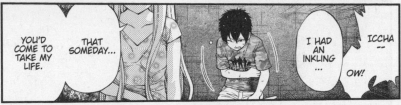

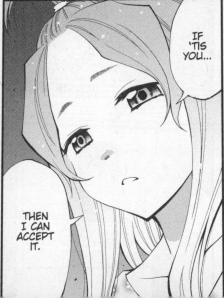

IF 'TIS YOU...

THEN I CAN ACCEPT IT.

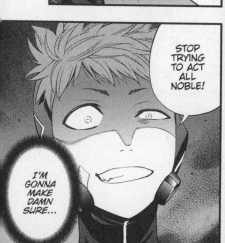

STOP TRYING TO ACT ALL NOBLE!

I'M GONNA MAKE DAMN SURE...

THAT YOU DIE!!!
WHOOSH
SAYA, I'VE KEPT YOU WAITING.
NOW...
I GO TO YOU.

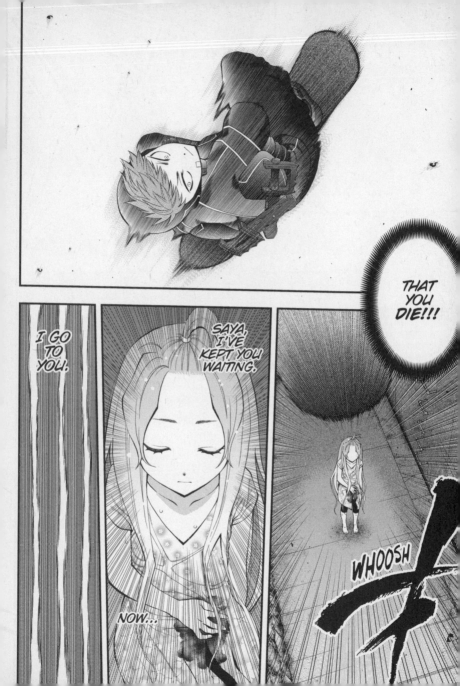

NGH...
CRACKLE
CRACKLE
GEH!
CRACKLE
YOU IDIOT!
CRACKLE
YOU'RE STILL GONNA GET IN MY WAY?!
WHIRRR
KA-THWAM

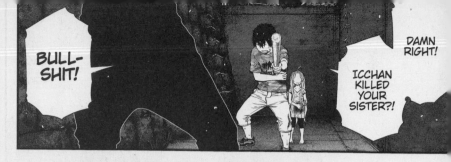

BULL-SHIT!

DAMN RIGHT!

ICCHAN KILLED YOUR SISTER?!

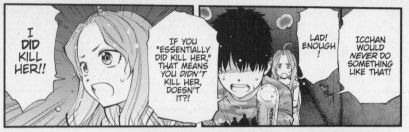

I DID KILL HER!!

IF YOU "ESSENTIALLY DID KILL HER," THAT MEANS YOU *DIDN'T* KILL HER, DOESN'T IT?!

LAD! ENOUGH!

ICCHAN WOULD *NEVER* DO SOMETHING LIKE THAT!

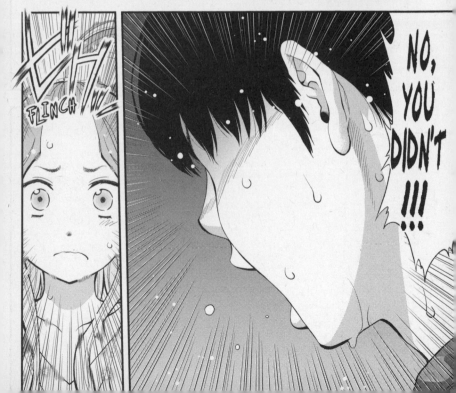

NO, YOU DIDN'T!!!

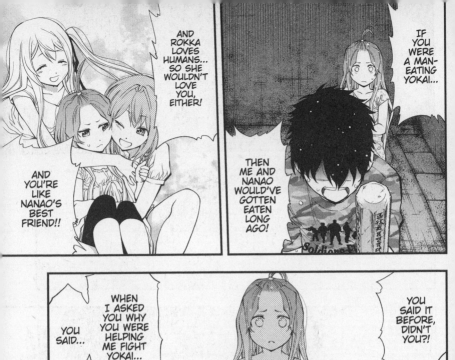

AND ROKKA LOVES HUMANS... SO SHE WOULDN'T LOVE YOU, EITHER!

AND YOU'RE LIKE NANAO'S BEST FRIEND!!

IF YOU WERE A MAN-EATING YOKAI...

THEN ME AND NANAO WOULD'VE GOTTEN EATEN LONG AGO!

WHEN I ASKED YOU WHY YOU WERE HELPING ME FIGHT YOKAI...

YOU SAID...

YOU SAID IT BEFORE, DIDN'T YOU?!

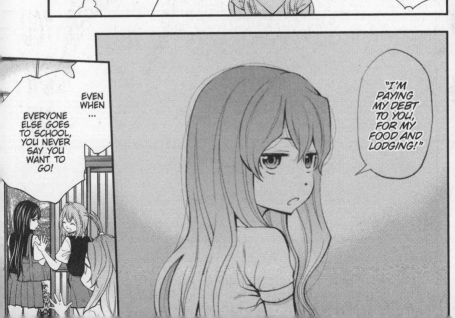

EVEN WHEN...

EVERYONE ELSE GOES TO SCHOOL, YOU NEVER SAY YOU WANT TO GO!

"I'M PAYING MY DEBT TO YOU, FOR MY FOOD AND LODGING!"

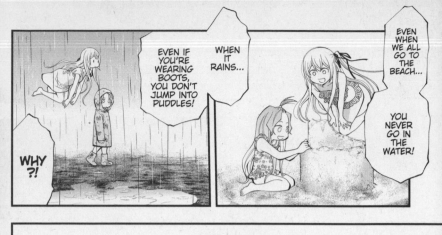

EVEN IF YOU'RE WEARING BOOTS, YOU DON'T JUMP INTO PUDDLES!

WHEN IT RAINS...

EVEN WHEN WE ALL GO TO THE BEACH...

YOU NEVER GO IN THE WATER!

WHY ?!

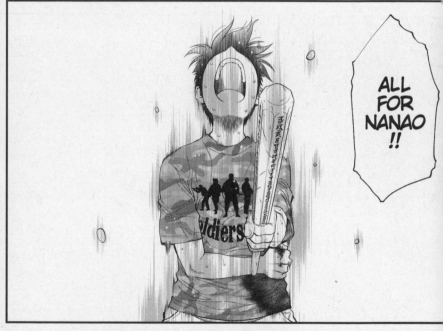

ALL FOR NANAO !!

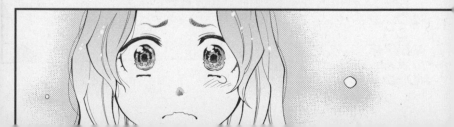

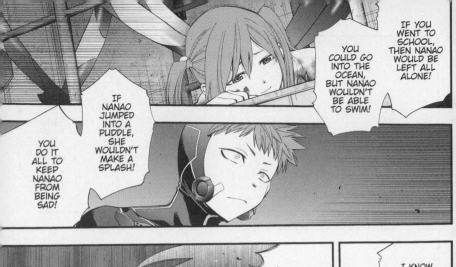

IF YOU WENT TO SCHOOL, THEN NANAO WOULD BE LEFT ALL ALONE!

YOU COULD GO INTO THE OCEAN, BUT NANAO WOULDN'T BE ABLE TO SWIM!

IF NANAO JUMPED INTO A PUDDLE, SHE WOULDN'T MAKE A SPLASH!

YOU DO IT ALL TO KEEP NANAO FROM BEING SAD!

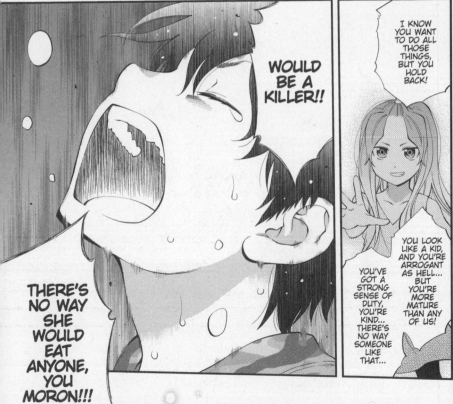

WOULD BE A KILLER!!

THERE'S NO WAY SHE WOULD EAT ANYONE, YOU MORON!!!

I KNOW YOU WANT TO DO ALL THOSE THINGS, BUT YOU HOLD BACK!

YOU LOOK LIKE A KID, AND YOU'RE ARROGANT AS HELL... BUT YOU'RE MORE MATURE THAN ANY OF US!

YOU'VE GOT A STRONG SENSE OF DUTY, YOU'RE KIND... THERE'S NO WAY SOMEONE LIKE THAT...

......
SOB...
I...
TRUST YOU!
NO MATTER WHAT THIS GUY SAYS.
EVEN IF...
YOU SAY YOU DID IT.
I TRUST YOU, ICCHAN!!

I TRUST THAT MAKABE ICHIE...
IS A YOKAI WHO LOVES HUMANS...
AND CAN BECOME FRIENDS WITH HUMANS!
LAD...

SO... COME HERE...
ICCHAN!

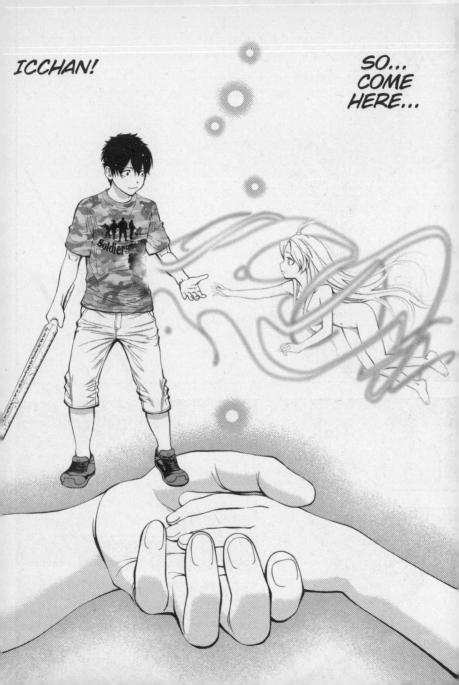

WHOA!
KIIII
ACK!!
EEK! WHAT?!
ZU ZU
HEY...
ZU
FUWA
WHAT NOW?!

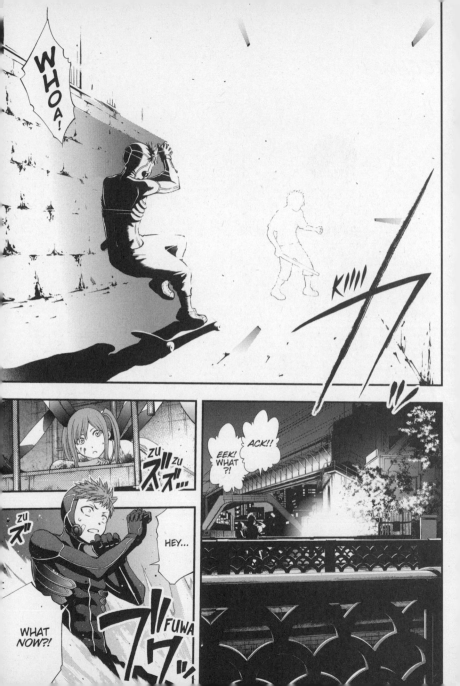

ZU
ズ
ZU
ズ
ZU
ズ
ZU
ズ
ZU
ズ

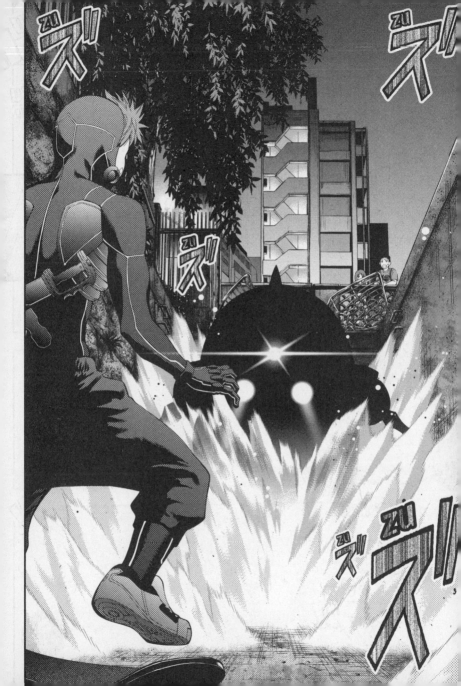

Zu
Zu
WH...
Zu
Zu
WHOA!
Zu
Zu
HOLD ON A MINUTE!!
Zu
75
Fusing with Icchan!! ♪

75
Fusing with Icchan!! ♪
ZUZUUUN
ズズズン

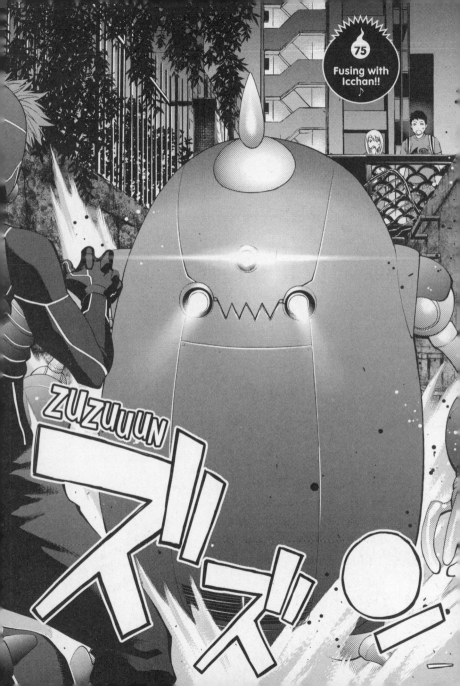

WHAT THE HELL IS THAT?!!
ドドド
WHAT IN THE DICKENS IS THIS?!!
BA-BAM!
HUH?!
ARE THEY FILMING A MOVIE?
WHOA!
THAT ROBOT'S SO CUTE!
A ROBOT?!
A ROBOT?!!
ME AND ICCHAN TURNED INTO A ROBOT?!!
CEASE YOUR BABBLING!!

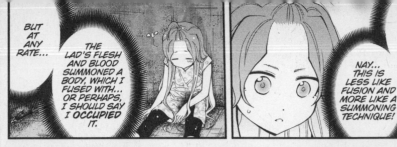

BUT AT ANY RATE...

THE LAD'S FLESH AND BLOOD SUMMONED A BODY, WHICH I FUSED WITH... OR PERHAPS, I SHOULD SAY I OCCUPIED IT.

SO THIS IS ETHE-REAL FUSION?!

NAY... THIS IS LESS LIKE FUSION AND MORE LIKE A SUMMONING TECHNIQUE!

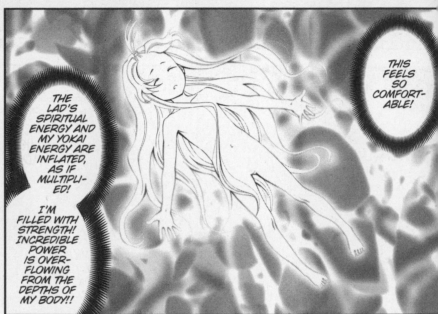

THE LAD'S SPIRITUAL ENERGY AND MY YOKAI ENERGY ARE INFLATED, AS IF MULTIPLI-ED!

I'M FILLED WITH STRENGTH! INCREDIBLE POWER IS OVER-FLOWING FROM THE DEPTHS OF MY BODY!!

THIS FEELS SO COMFORT-ABLE!

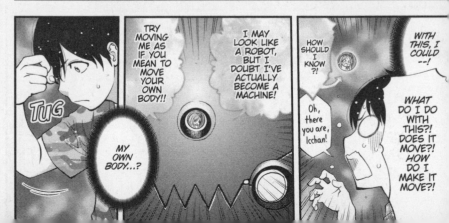

TRY MOVING ME AS IF YOU MEAN TO MOVE YOUR OWN BODY!!

MY OWN BODY...?

I MAY LOOK LIKE A ROBOT, BUT I DOUBT I'VE ACTUALLY BECOME A MACHINE!

HOW SHOULD I KNOW?!

Oh, there you are, Icchan!

WITH THIS, I COULD --!

WHAT DO I DO WITH THIS?! DOES IT MOVE?! HOW DO I MAKE IT MOVE?!

TUG

WHIRR WHIRR
WHIRR
HEY! I CAN MOVE YOU!
RIGHT! THEN...
LET'S DO THIS, LAD!!
YEAH!!
STOMP
TO-GETHER, WE CAN DO IT!!

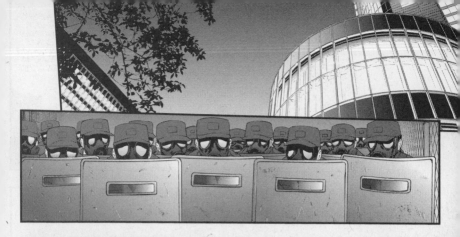

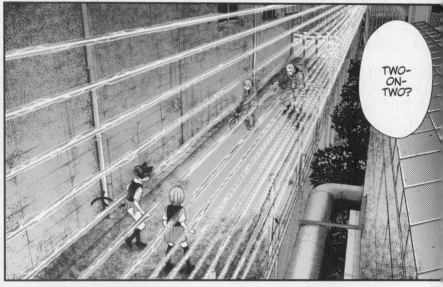

TWO-ON-TWO?

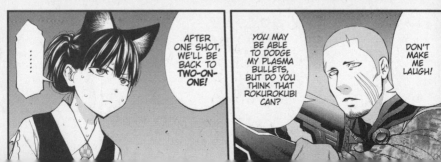

AFTER ONE SHOT, WE'LL BE BACK TO **TWO-ON-ONE!**

YOU MAY BE ABLE TO DODGE MY PLASMA BULLETS, BUT DO YOU THINK THAT ROKUROKUBI CAN?

DON'T MAKE ME LAUGH!

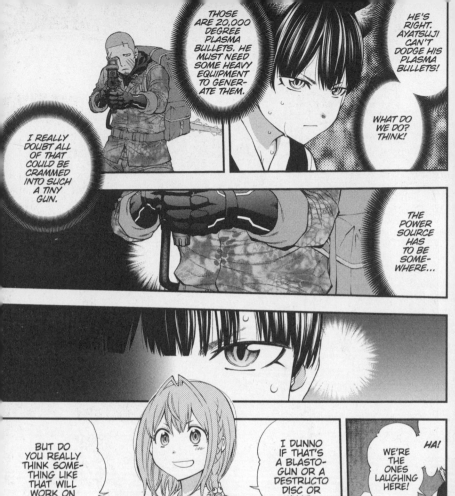

THOSE ARE 20,000 DEGREE PLASMA BULLETS. HE MUST NEED SOME HEAVY EQUIPMENT TO GENERATE THEM.

HE'S RIGHT. AYATSUJI CAN'T DODGE HIS PLASMA BULLETS!

WHAT DO WE DO? THINK!

I REALLY DOUBT ALL OF THAT COULD BE CRAMMED INTO SUCH A TINY GUN.

THE POWER SOURCE HAS TO BE SOME- WHERE...

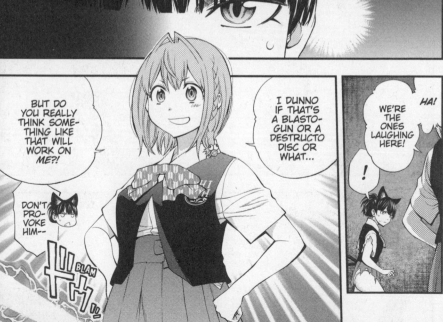

BUT DO YOU REALLY THINK SOME- THING LIKE THAT WILL WORK ON ME?!

I DUNNO IF THAT'S A BLASTO- GUN OR A DESTRUCTO DISC OR WHAT...

HA!

WE'RE THE ONES LAUGHING HERE!

!

DON'T PRO- VOKE HIM--

BLAM

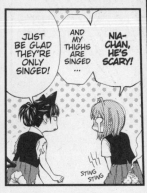

JUST BE GLAD THEY'RE ONLY SINGED!

AND MY THIGHS ARE SINGED...

NIA-CHAN, HE'S SCARY!

STING STING

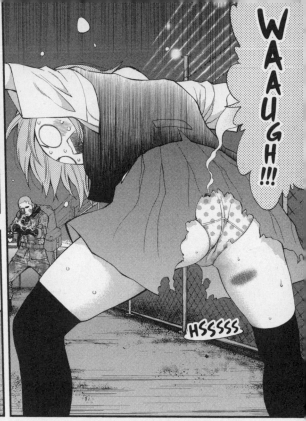

WAAUGH!!!

HSSSSS

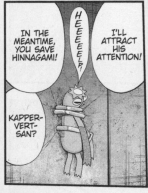

IN THE MEANTIME, YOU SAVE HINNAGAMI!

HEEEEEL?

I'LL ATTRACT HIS ATTENTION!

KAPPER-VERT-SAN?

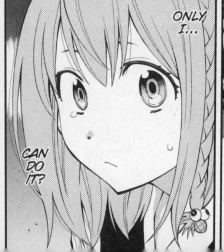

ONLY I...

CAN DO IT?

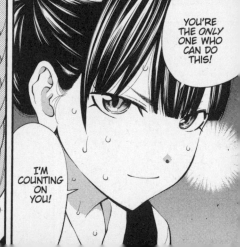

YOU'RE THE ONLY ONE WHO CAN DO THIS!

I'M COUNTING ON YOU!

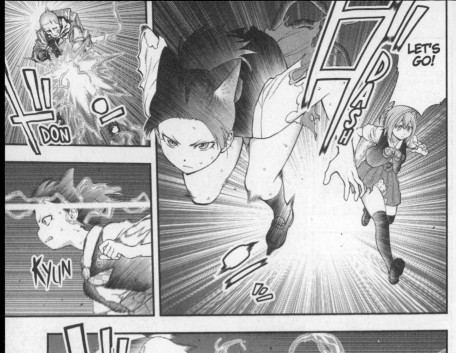

LET'S GO!

DON

KYUN

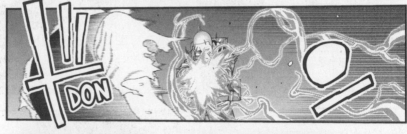

DON

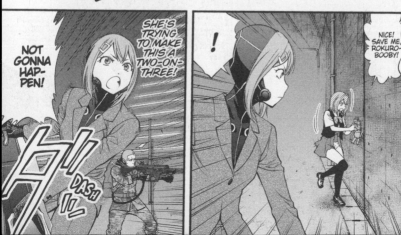

SHE'S TRYING TO MAKE THIS A TWO-ON-THREE!

NOT GONNA HAP-PEN!

DASH

!

NICE! SAVE ME, ROKURO-BOOBY!

KAP-PER-VERT-SAN!

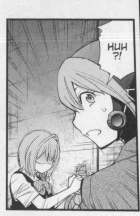

HUH ?!

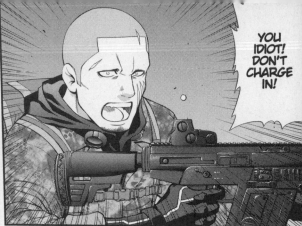

YOU IDIOT! DON'T CHARGE IN!

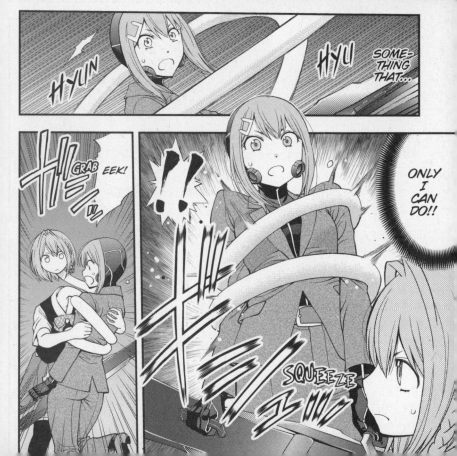

HYUN

HYU

SOME-THING THAT...

GRAB

EEK!

ONLY I CAN DO!!

SQUEEZE

PUT HER IN MY LINE OF FIRE!

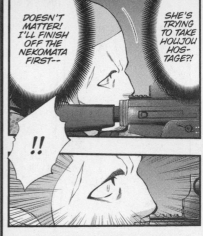

DOESN'T MATTER! I'LL FINISH OFF THE NEKOMATA FIRST--

SHE'S TRYING TO TAKE HOLIJOU HOSTAGE?!

!!

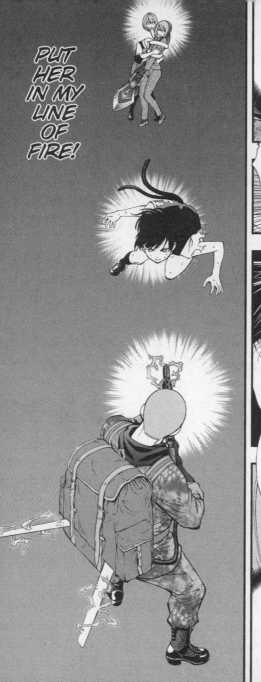

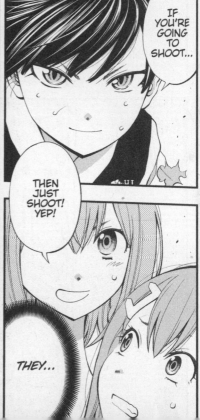

IF YOU'RE GOING TO SHOOT...

THEN JUST SHOOT! YEP!

THEY...

SHING
SHE CUT MY HIGH-VOLTAGE TRANS-FORMER CABLE!
SHE GOT ME!
NOW I CAN'T HEAT UP THE PLASMA!
BUT...
THWACK

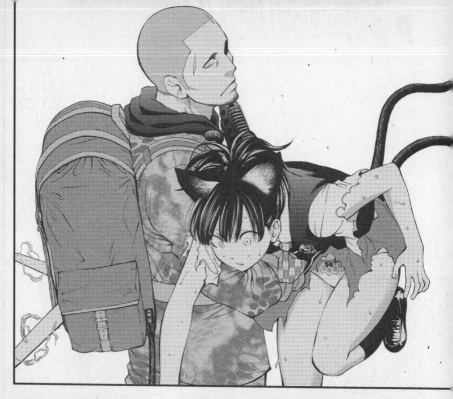

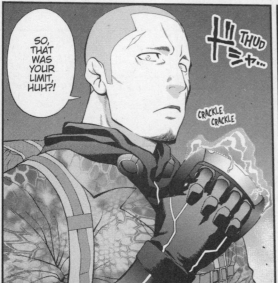

SO, THAT WAS YOUR LIMIT, HUH?!

ト リ THUD
ニャ…

CRACKLE
CRACKLE

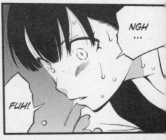

NGH
...

FUH!

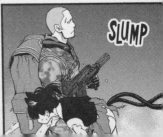

SLUMP

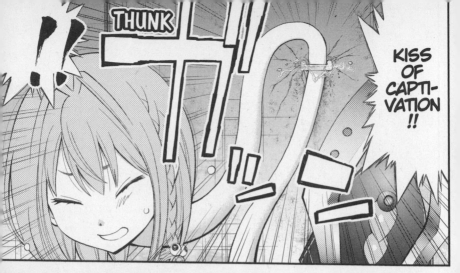

THUNK

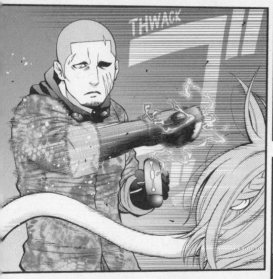

THWACK

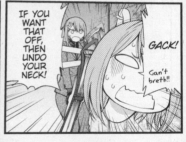

IF YOU WANT THAT OFF, THEN UNDO YOUR NECK!

GACK!

Can't breth!!

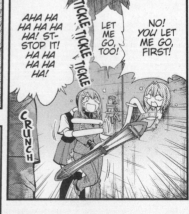

AHA HA HA HA HA! ST-STOP IT! HA HA HA HA HA!

TICKLE TICKLE TICKLE

LET ME GO, TOO!

NO! YOU! YOU LET ME GO, FIRST!

CRUNCH

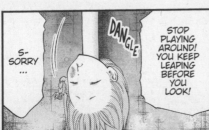

DANGLE

S-SORRY...

STOP PLAYING AROUND! YOU KEEP LEAPING BEFORE YOU LOOK!

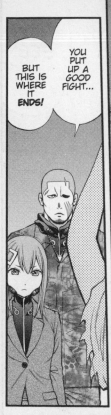

BUT THIS IS WHERE IT **ENDS!**

YOU PUT UP A GOOD FIGHT...

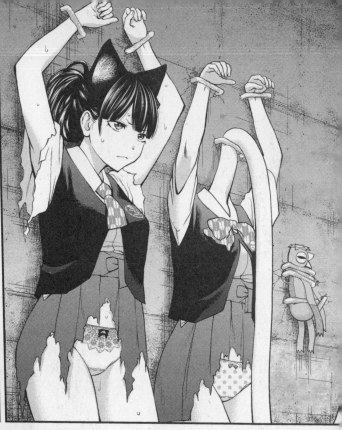

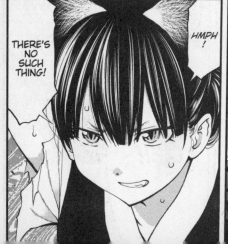

THERE'S NO SUCH THING!

HMPH!

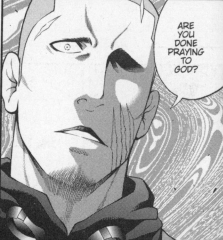

ARE YOU DONE PRAYING TO GOD?

I SEE.
CRACKLE
THEN DIE!!
NGH!
SO THIS IS IT!
BUT...
I WANT TO SAVE AYATSUJI, AT LEAST!
AT LEAST HER!!
WHAT SHOULD I DO...?
TOSS
SHURURU
!
NYUUR

DO-BAN!
CRACKLE CRACKLE
HNN!
CRACKLE
NGH!
CRACKLE CRACKLE
ZU ZA ZA ZA ZAAA
ズザザザザーッ
......
WHAT THE HELL ARE YOU?!

WHAT AM I, YOU ASK?
......!
MY ANSWER: A MAN IN THE SEASON OF HIS PRIME!
A MAN AT THE PEAK OF RIPE PERFECTION!
DRIPPING WITH JUICY STYLE!
RIPENED SLOWLY ON THE TREE, AGED LIKE FINE WINE!
THE SWEET-ASSED GENTLEMAN, THE KAKI-OTOKO!!
TUG
KAKIOTOKO
PARDON...
THE INTRUSION!!
LOOM

76
All You've Got...!
♪

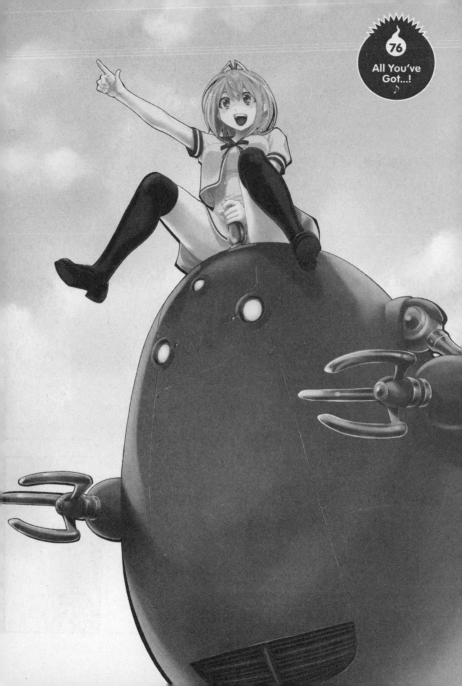

LOOM
DRIPPING WITH JUICY STYLE!
THE SWEET-ASSED GENTLEMAN, THE KAKI-OTOKO!
PARDON...
THE INTRUSION!
LOOM
LOOM
HNN?
TH-THE BUTT GUY?! WHY ARE YOU HERE?!
I'M NOT "THE BUTT GUY!" I'M KAKIOTOKO, OR "TAN-TAN KORORIN-SAMA"!
OH? SO IT'S YOU GUYS?
CLICK

YOU'RE THE REASON COMMANDO KARATE GIRL ASKED ME HERE?
NA...
GOOD GRIEF!
YOU YOKAI GIRLS ARE A REAL BOTHER!
NAGI-SAN!!
DON

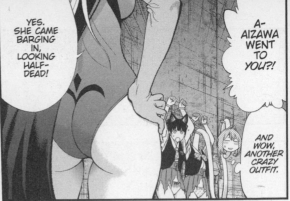

YES. SHE CAME BARGING IN, LOOKING HALF-DEAD!

A-AIZAWA WENT TO YOU?!

AND WOW, ANOTHER CRAZY OUTFIT.

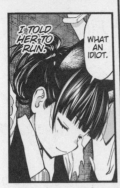

I TOLD HER TO RUN.

WHAT AN IDIOT.

.....

OH!

SHE TOOK THEM OFF HER-SELF, YEP!

WELL... IT'S A LONG STORY...

BY THE WAY, WHY WASN'T SHE WEARING UNDERWEAR?

NO, SHE DIDN'T!
I mean, she did, but...!

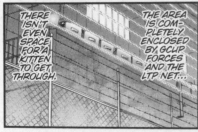

THERE ISN'T EVEN SPACE FOR A KITTEN TO GET THROUGH.

THE AREA IS COM-PLETELY ENCLOSED BY GCUP FORCES AND THE LTP NET...

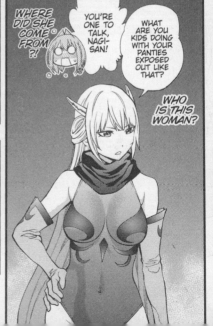

WHERE DID SHE COME FROM?!

YOU'RE ONE TO TALK, NAGI-SAN!

WHAT ARE YOU KIDS DOING WITH YOUR PANTIES EXPOSED OUT LIKE THAT?

WHO IS THIS WOMAN?

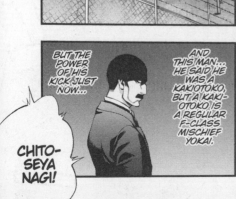

BUT THE POWER OF HIS KICK JUST NOW...

AND THIS MAN... HE SAID HE WAS A KAKIOTOKO, BUT A KAKI-OTOKO IS A REGULAR F-CLASS MISCHIEF YOKAI.

CHITO-SEYA NAGI!

THE COSPLAY FORTUNE-TELLER OF AKIBA!! SO YOU'VE *FINALLY* SHOWN YOURSELF!!
KA-CHK
YOUR TIME HAS COME! PREPARE YOURSELF!!
OH!
IT'S BEEN A LONG TIME, SAKURAKO!
YOU KNOW EACH OTHER?!
YES! WE'RE OLD FRIENDS!
LIKE *HELL* WE ARE!
I MAY THINK OF YOU AS AN ENEMY...
BUT I'VE NEVER *ONCE* THOUGHT OF YOU AS A FRIEND!
DON'T BE SO HARSH.
YOU'LL LOSE FRIENDS THAT WAY.
SHUT UP!
......
WELL...
IN THAT CASE, THIS IS PERFECT.

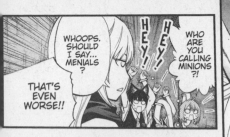

WHOOPS. SHOULD I SAY... MENIALS?

HEY!! HEY!! WHO ARE YOU CALLING MINIONS?!

THAT'S EVEN WORSE!!

I WAS JUST STARTING TO GET RATHER IRRITATED AT SEEING MY MINIONS BEING TORMENTED.

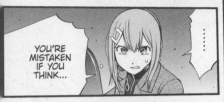

YOU'RE MISTAKEN IF YOU THINK...

......

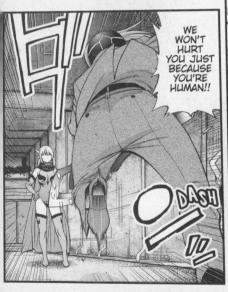

WE WON'T HURT YOU JUST BECAUSE YOU'RE HUMAN!!

DASH

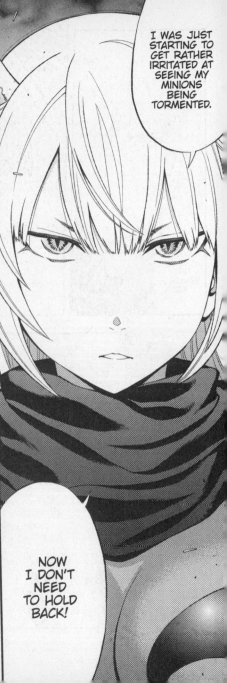

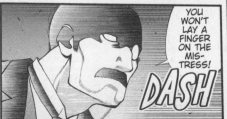

YOU WON'T LAY A FINGER ON THE MISTRESS!

DASH

NOW I DON'T NEED TO HOLD BACK!

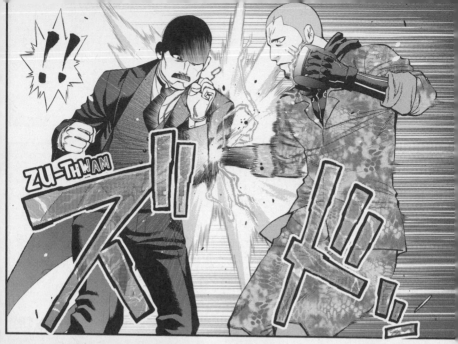

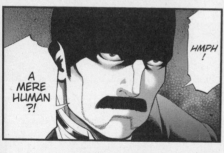

A MERE HUMAN?!

HMPH!

I'M YOUR OPPONENT!

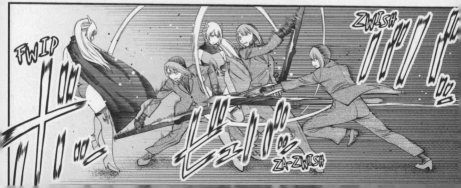

!

BECAUSE OF YOUR FATHER, AFTER ALL?

WAS IT...

SO THE RUMORS YOU'D JOINED GCUP WERE TRUE.

FWIP

SHUT UP! THAT'S GOT NOTHING TO DO WITH THIS!!

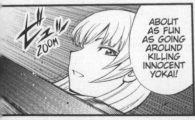

ZOOM

ABOUT AS FUN AS GOING AROUND KILLING INNOCENT YOKAI!

YES, IT IS!

ZWISH ZWISH

WHAT ABOUT YOU?! IS IT FUN, BEING A HUMAN WHO ACTS LIKE A YOKAI BOSS?!

ZA ZWISH

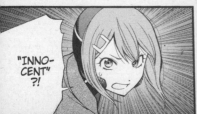

"INNOCENT"?!

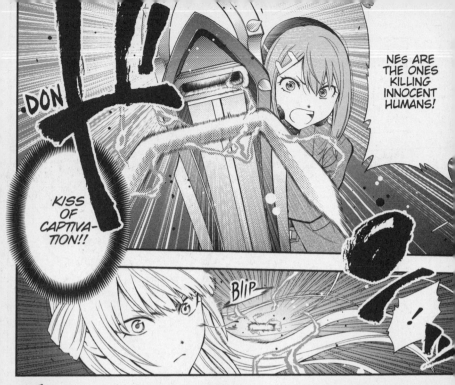

NES ARE THE ONES KILLING INNOCENT HUMANS!

KISS OF CAPTIVATION!!

-DON

BLIP

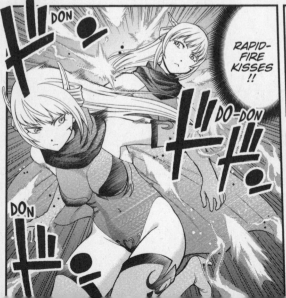

DON

RAPID-FIRE KISSES!!

DO-DON

DON

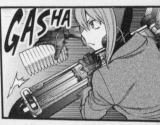

GASHA

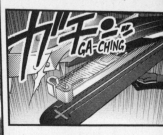

GA-CHING

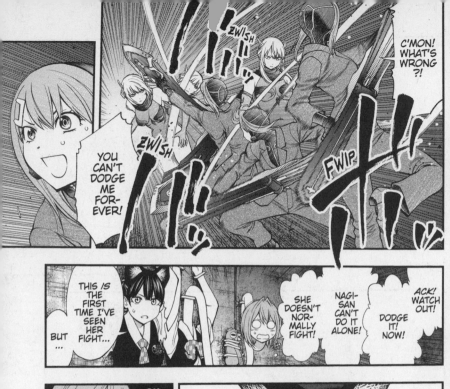

C'MON! WHAT'S WRONG ?!

ZWISH

ZWISH

FWIP

YOU CAN'T DODGE ME FOR-EVER!

THIS *IS* THE FIRST TIME I'VE SEEN HER FIGHT...

BUT...

SHE DOESN'T NOR-MALLY FIGHT!

NAGI-SAN CAN'T DO IT ALONE!

DODGE IT! NOW!

ACK! WATCH OUT!

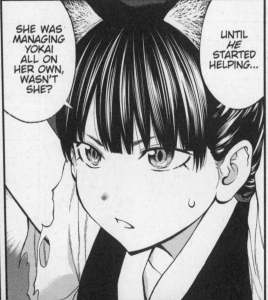

Oh...

SHE WAS MANAGING YOKAI ALL ON HER OWN, WASN'T SHE?

UNTIL *HE* STARTED HELPING...

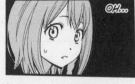

TRUE.

SHFF

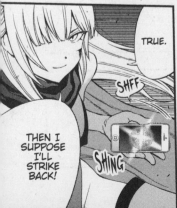

THEN I SUPPOSE I'LL STRIKE BACK!

SHING

SHWOO

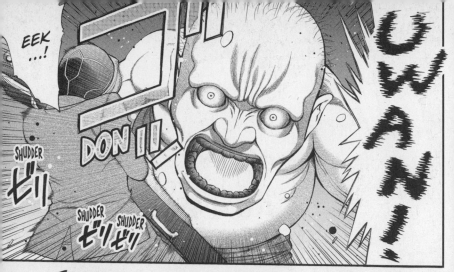

EEK ....!

DON !!!

SHUDDER
ビリ

SHUDDER
ビリ

SHUDDER
ビリ

UWAN!

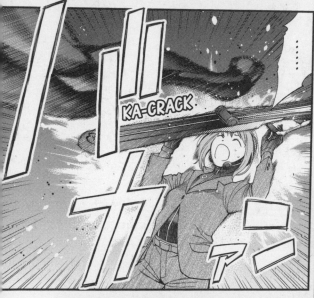

KA-CRACK

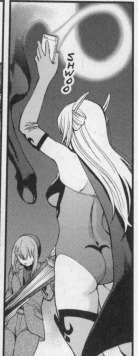

SHWOO

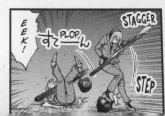

EEK!
PLOP
すとーん

STAGGER

STEP

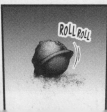

ROLL ROLL

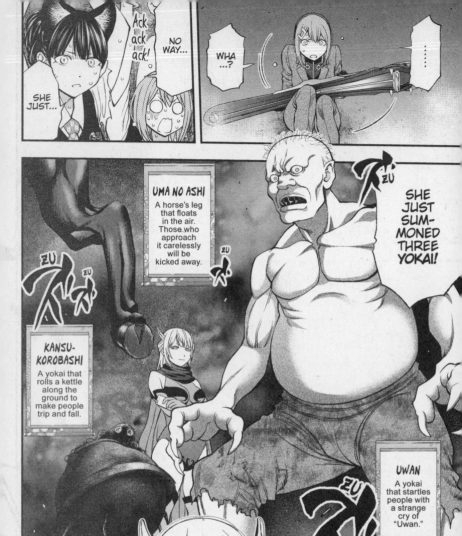

Ack ack ack!

NO WAY...

WHA ...?

....

SHE JUST...

UMA NO ASHI
A horse's leg that floats in the air. Those who approach it carelessly will be kicked away.

KANSU-KOROBASHI
A yokai that rolls a kettle along the ground to make people trip and fall.

SHE JUST SUMMONED THREE YOKAI!

UWAN
A yokai that startles people with a strange cry of "Uwan."

THE KAKIOTOKO ISN'T THE ONLY YOKAI WHO SERVES ME.

HEH HEH! ♪

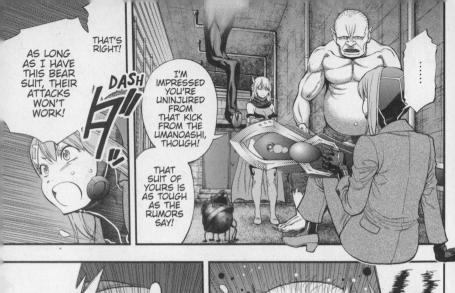

AS LONG AS I HAVE THIS BEAR SUIT, THEIR ATTACKS WON'T WORK!

THAT'S RIGHT!

DASH

I'M IMPRESSED YOU'RE UNINJURED FROM THAT KICK FROM THE UMANOASHI, THOUGH!

THAT SUIT OF YOURS IS AS TOUGH AS THE RUMORS SAY!

......

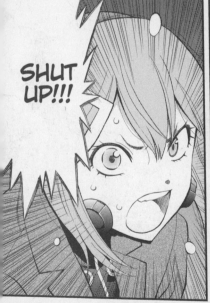

SHUT UP!!!

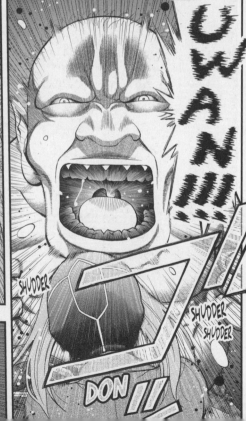

UWAN!!!

SHUDDER

SHUDDER
SHUDDER

DON

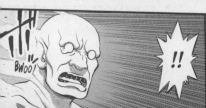

BWOO!

!!

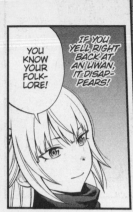

YOU KNOW YOUR FOLKLORE!

IF YOU YELL RIGHT BACK AT AN UWAN, IT DISAPPEARS!

OH?

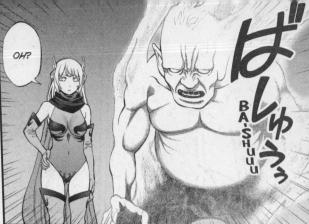

BA-SHUUU

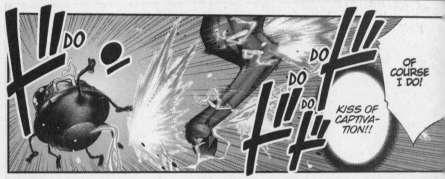

DO

DO

DO

DO

DO

OF COURSE I DO!

KISS OF CAPTIVATION!!

IS THIS ALL YOU'VE GOT?!

YOU MAY BE ABLE TO SUMMON NES, BUT THEY'RE ALL SMALL FRY!

HA!

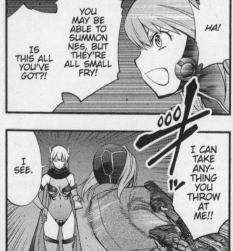

I SEE.

I CAN TAKE ANYTHING YOU THROW AT ME!!

!

SHUUU

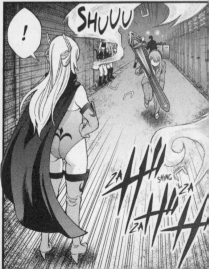

ZA

SHING

ZA

ZA

YOU'RE BETTER THAN I THOUGHT!
FLICK
THEN THERE'S NO HELPING IT...
I DIDN'T WANT TO USE THIS, BUT...
SPIIIN
FLASH
I SUPPOSE I'LL GO WITH SOMETHING A LITTLE BIGGER!
?!
I ORDER YOU, IN THE NAME OF SUOU BYAKUREN...
COME FORTH!

CHOMP
WARAI-HANNYA!!!
CRUNCH CRUNCH

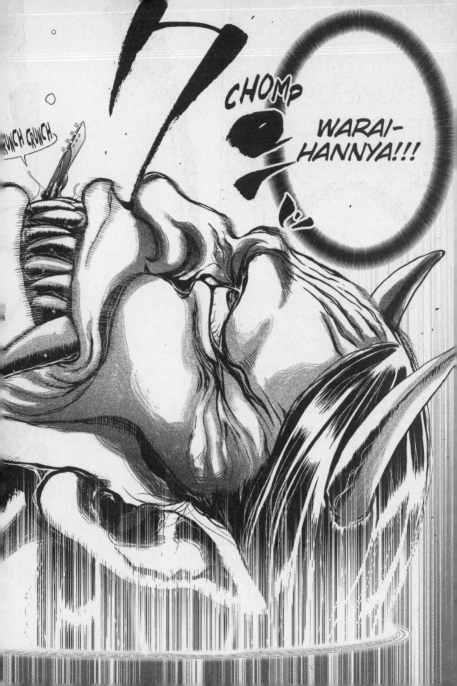

HEH! HEH! HEH! HEH! HEH! HEH!
HEH! HEH! HEH! HEH! HEH! HEH!
MUNCH MUNCH
CRUNCH CRUNCH
......
Hmm?
MUNCH
PTOO!
THWACK
SPLAT

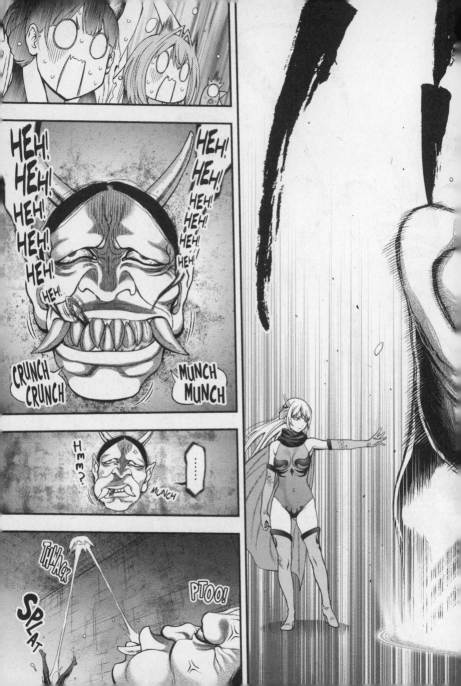

AH ...
HM.
GUH!

YOU SAID YOU COULD TAKE ANYTHING, SO I CAME UP WITH A BIG ONE.
WAS IT A LITTLE MUCH?

WELL...
LOOKS LIKE THAT'S ALL YOU'VE GOT!
TONK

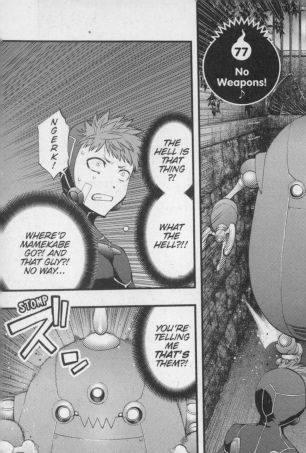

NGERK!

THE HELL IS THAT THING?!

WHAT THE HELL?!!

WHERE'D MAMEKABE GO?! AND THAT GUY?! NO WAY...

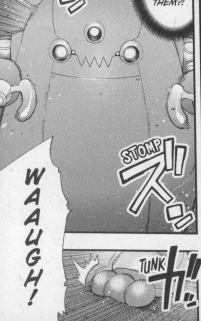

STOMP ズ!!

YOU'RE TELLING ME THAT'S THEM?!

STOMP ズ!!

WAAUGH!

TUNK ザ!!

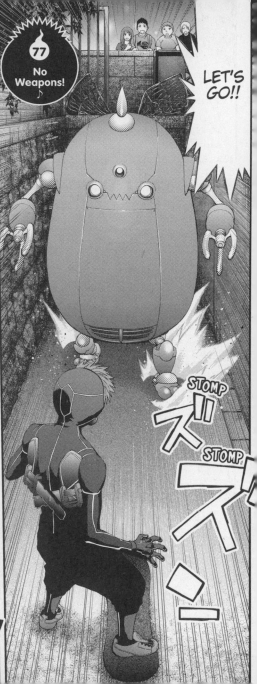

77

No Weapons! ♪

LET'S GO!!

STOMP ズ!!

STOMP ズ!!

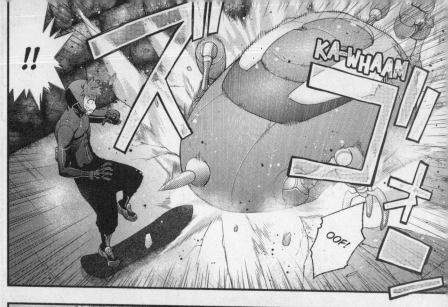

!!

KA-WHAAM

OOF!

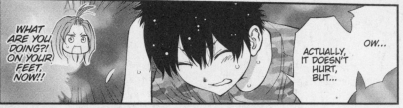

WHAT ARE YOU DOING?! ON YOUR FEET, NOW!!

OW...

ACTUALLY, IT DOESN'T HURT, BUT...

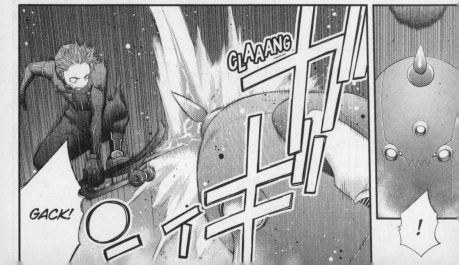

GLAAANG

GACK!

!

I'LL FIGURE OUT WHAT THE HELL JUST HAPPENED LATER!
FEH!
RIGHT NOW, I'M JUST GONNA TAKE THIS BIG, SLOW THING DOWN...
AND SMASH IT UP GOOD!!!
WAK
THWACK
WAK
WAK
WAK
......
SKRRRSHHH
HUNH!
HEY, SLOW-ASS--
!

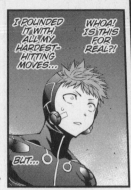

I POUNDED IT WITH ALL MY HARDEST-HITTING MOVES...

WHOA! IS THIS FOR REAL?!

BUT...

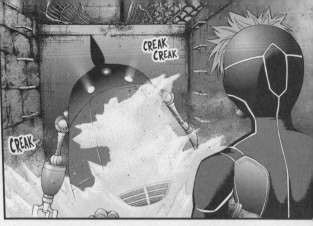

CREAK CREAK

CREAK

CREAK CREAK

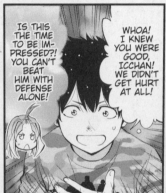

IS THIS THE TIME TO BE IMPRESSED?! YOU CAN'T BEAT HIM WITH DEFENSE ALONE!

WHOA! I KNEW YOU WERE GOOD, ICCHAN! WE DIDN'T GET HURT AT ALL!

HE DOESN'T EVEN HAVE A SCRATCH!!

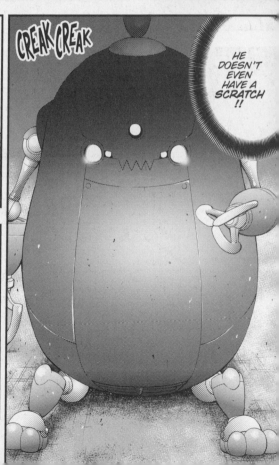

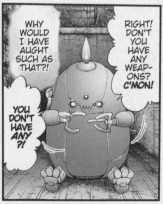

WHY WOULD I HAVE AUGHT SUCH AS THAT?!

RIGHT! DON'T YOU HAVE ANY WEAPONS? C'MON!

YOU DON'T HAVE ANY?!

SO, THEN...
HOW ABOUT THIS?!
WHACK
NO, YOU FOOL! NOT THA--
SNAP
UH...
KCHK
!
HE'S BACKING UP! IT COULDN'T BE...
SHIIII
ARC JET THRUST-ERS, ACTIVATE!
NOT GOOD!!
THIS'LL BE MY THIRD GO!
VRRRRR
I'LL GIVE 'EM MY FINAL SHOT!!
IING
HONEY! YOU CAN'T LET THAT HIT YOU!!
......
IT CAME OFF...?
HUH?

HEDGEHOG BULLET!!!
ZU-DOOOOON

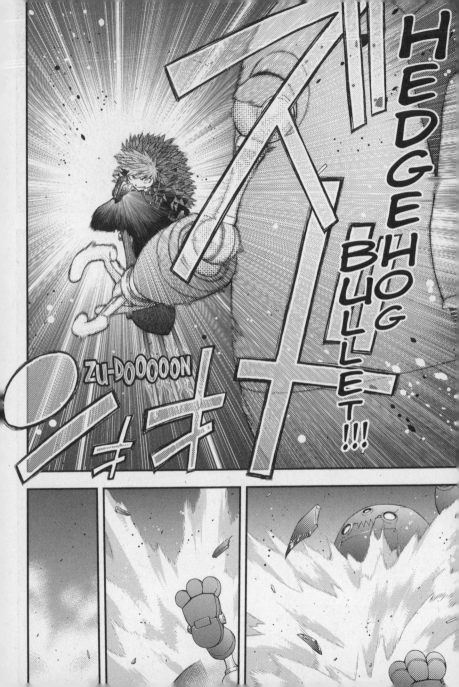

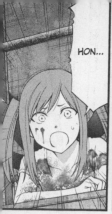

HON...

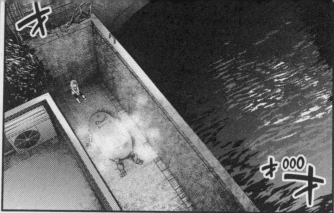

✱000

!!

← Tiny

SHUUU

WOW!

AFTER TAKING AN ATTACK LIKE THAT...?!

WAIT.

WHAT HAPPENED TO SPIKY?

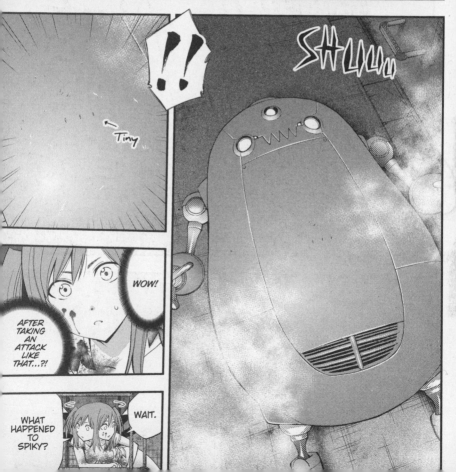

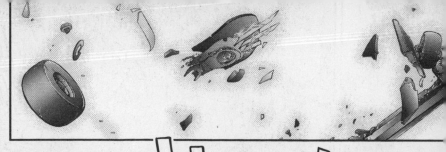

KA-BAM

YEEEK!!

HUH?!

WHAT WAS THAT?

CLATTER

CLATTER

GAH!

THUD

THA-THUD

I PLAY HORA

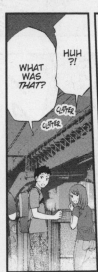

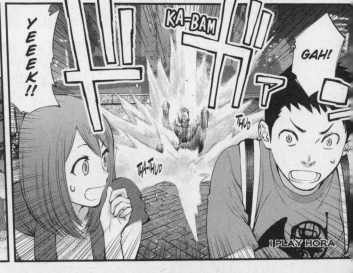

AND THE KNIFE, TOO.

MY BOARD IS IN PIECES...

HEY? YOU OKAY, MAN?

WAIT, AREN'T THEY FILMING NOW?

Is it okay to talk to him?

CLATTER

WAY...

NO...

CLANG

THUNK

CLATTER CLATTER

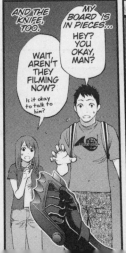

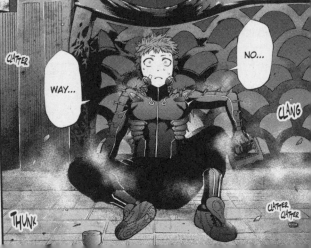

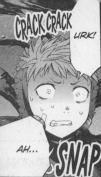

CRACK CRACK

URK!

AH...

SNAP

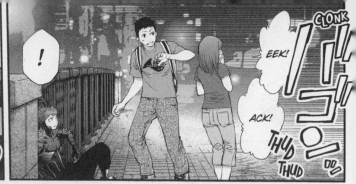

!

EEK!

ACK!

THUD THUD

CLONK

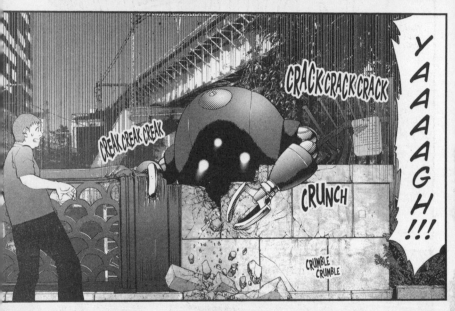

CREAK CREAK CREAK

CRACK CRACK CRACK

CRUNCH

CRUMBLE CRUMBLE

YAAAAGH!!!

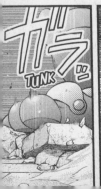

TUNK

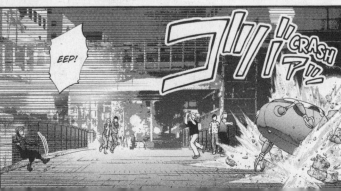

EEP!

CRASH

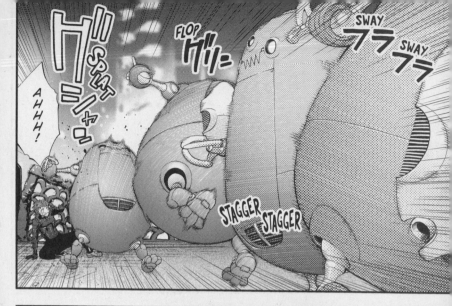

AHHH!

FLOP

SWAY SWAY

STAGGER STAGGER

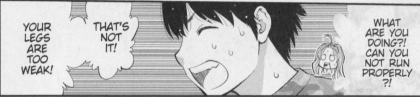

WHAT ARE YOU DOING?! CAN YOU NOT RUN PROPERLY?!

THAT'S NOT IT!

YOUR LEGS ARE TOO WEAK!

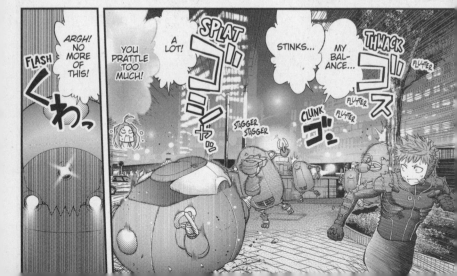

ARGH! NO MORE OF THIS!

FLASH

YOU PRATTLE TOO MUCH!

A LOT!

SPLAT

STINKS...

MY BAL-ANCE...

THWACK

FLUTTER

STAGGER STAGGER

CLUNK

FLUTTER

FLUTTER

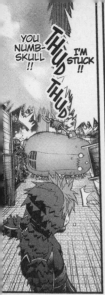

YOU NUMB-SKULL!!

THUD THUD

I'M STUCK!!

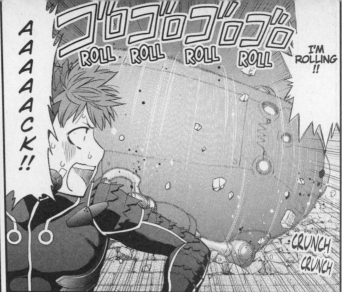

AAAAACK!!

ゴロゴロゴロゴロ
ROLL ROLL ROLL ROLL

I'M ROLLING!!

CRUNCH CRUNCH

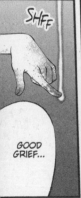

SHFF

GOOD GRIEF...

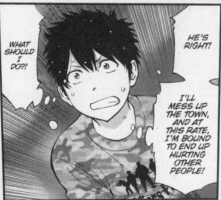

WHAT SHOULD I DO?!

HE'S RIGHT!

I'LL MESS UP THE TOWN, AND AT THIS RATE, I'M BOUND TO END UP HURTING OTHER PEOPLE!

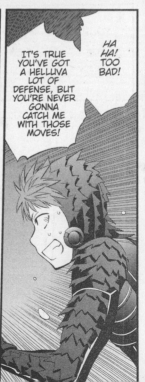

IT'S TRUE YOU'VE GOT A HELLUVA LOT OF DEFENSE, BUT YOU'RE NEVER GONNA CATCH ME WITH THOSE MOVES!

HA HA! TOO BAD!

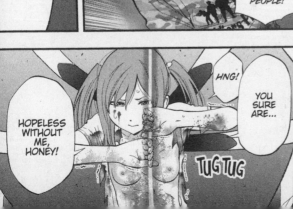

HNG!

HOPELESS WITHOUT ME, HONEY!

YOU SURE ARE...

TUG TUG

GWOO
!!
OOOOO
OOO
OOO
OOO
OOO
THIS IS HIME-CHAN'S...
WH-WHAT IS THIS PLACE?!
OOO

YOU CAN DO IT...

THIS'LL LAST ABOUT A MINUTE AT MOST.

WITH MY POWER WHERE IT IS NOW...

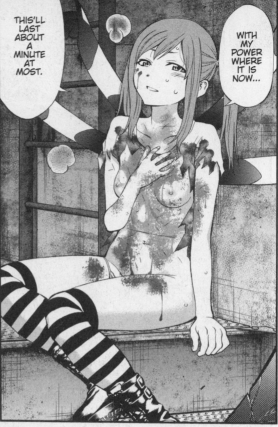

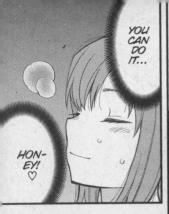

HON-EY! ♥

YOU, IDIOT! FORCING YOURSELF WHEN YOU CAN BARELY HOLD IT TOGETHER...

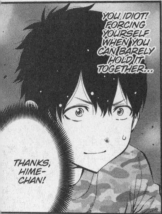

THANKS, HIME-CHAN!

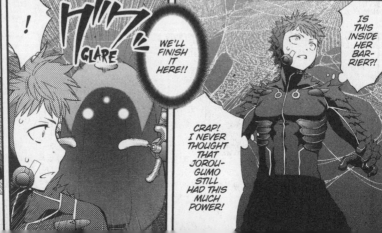

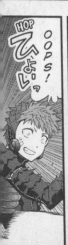

HOP

OOPS!

!

グッ GLARE

WE'LL FINISH IT HERE!!

IS THIS INSIDE HER BAR-RIER?!

CRAP! I NEVER THOUGHT THAT JOROU-GUMO STILL HAD THIS MUCH POWER!

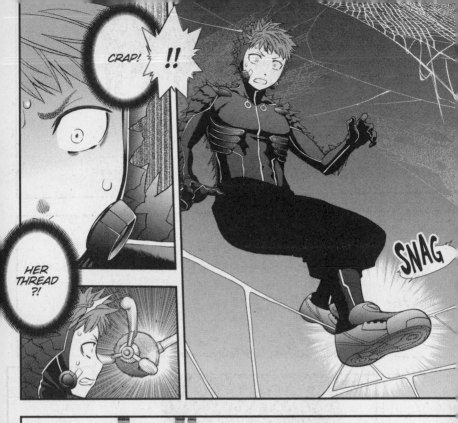

CRAP!

!!

HER THREAD ?!

SNAG

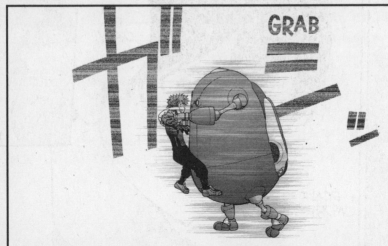

GRAB

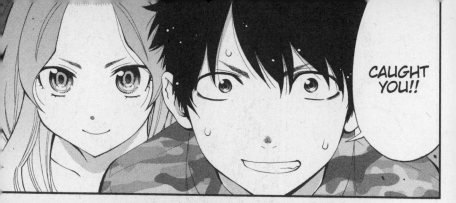

CAUGHT YOU!!

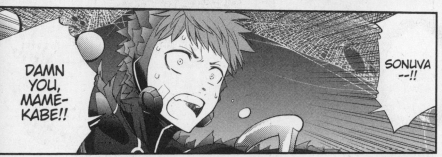

DAMN YOU, MAME-KABE!!

SONUVA--!!

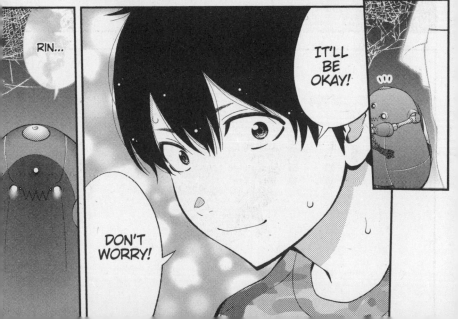

RIN...

IT'LL BE OKAY!

DON'T WORRY!

I'M ALIVE!
AND... I'LL FULFILL MY PROMISE TO SAYA!!
HER...
PROMISE ...?
CRACK...

KRRRRSH
WHA ...
WAIT ...!
WE'VE...
WON!!

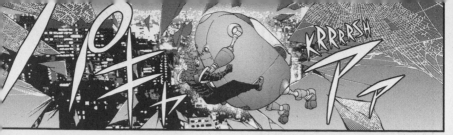

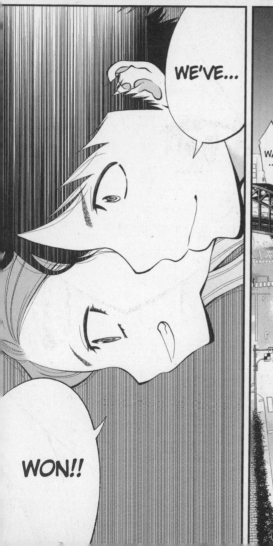

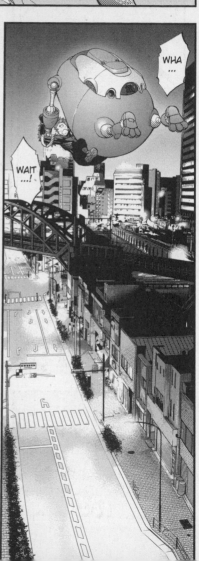

WAAAAGH!!!...
絶破断撃
MOUNTAIN-FALL...
KA-BLAAAM
鎧壁超圧殺!!!!!...
SMASHING ARMOR-WALL DEATH PRESS!!!!!!

絶破断撃
MOUNTAIN-FALL...
DO-THWAM
SMASHING ARMOR-WALL DEATH PRESS!!!!!
鎧壁超圧殺!!!!!
78 I Know She Was There...♪
OOO
O
CLATTER
CLATTER CLATTER
OOO
PLINK
PLINK
OOO

78
I Know She Was There... ♪
CLANK
CLATTER CLATTER
CLANK

HAAH! HAAH!
YOU...
DAMN...
HAAH!

WE'VE WON THIS ONE!
......
オooo
SLUMP
オoooo
オ
oooオ

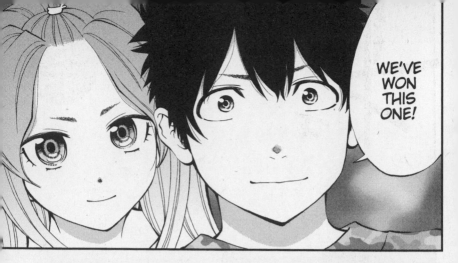

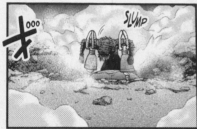

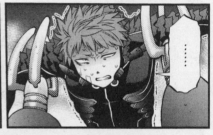

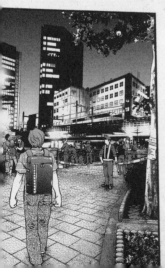

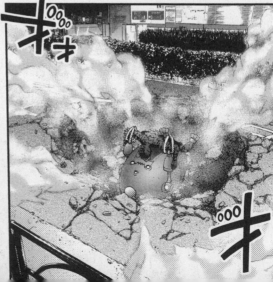

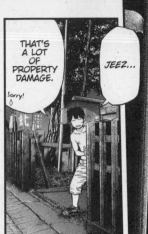

JEEZ...

THAT'S A LOT OF PROPERTY DAMAGE.

Sorry!

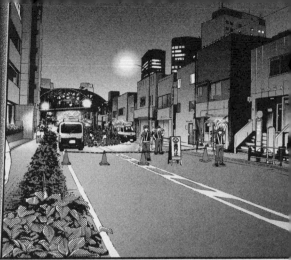

HE'S STILL UNCON-SCIOUS.

HOW IS HE?

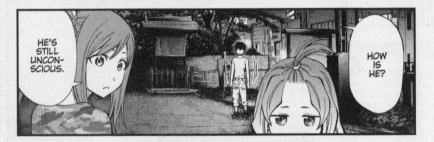

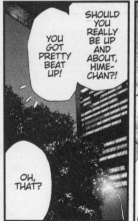

SHOULD YOU REALLY BE UP AND ABOUT, HIME-CHAN?!

YOU GOT PRETTY BEAT UP!

OH, THAT?

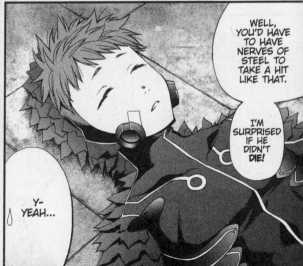

WELL, YOU'D HAVE TO HAVE NERVES OF STEEL TO TAKE A HIT LIKE THAT.

I'M SURPRISED IF HE DIDN'T DIE!

Y-YEAH...

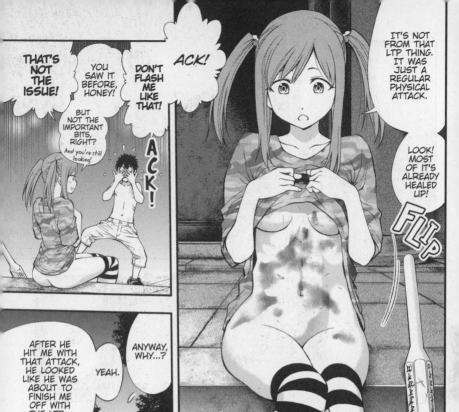

IT'S NOT FROM THAT LTP THING. IT WAS JUST A REGULAR PHYSICAL ATTACK.

LOOK! MOST OF IT'S ALREADY HEALED UP!

FLIP

THAT'S NOT THE ISSUE!

YOU SAW IT BEFORE, HONEY!

DON'T FLASH ME LIKE THAT!

ACK!

BUT NOT THE IMPORTANT BITS, RIGHT?

And you're still looking!

ACK!

ACK!

AFTER HE HIT ME WITH THAT ATTACK, HE LOOKED LIKE HE WAS ABOUT TO FINISH ME OFF WITH THE LTP...

YEAH.

ANYWAY, WHY...?

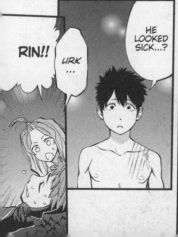

RIN!!

URK...

HE LOOKED SICK...?

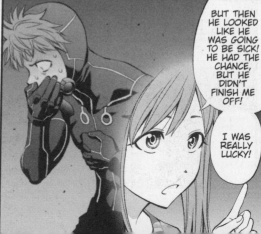

BUT THEN HE LOOKED LIKE HE WAS GOING TO BE SICK! HE HAD THE CHANCE, BUT HE DIDN'T FINISH ME OFF!

I WAS REALLY LUCKY!

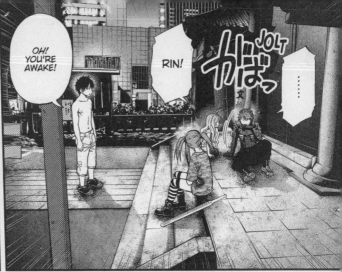

ANSWER ME!

OH! YOU'RE AWAKE!

RIN!

JOLT
かばっ

......

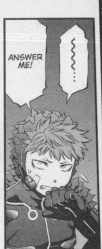

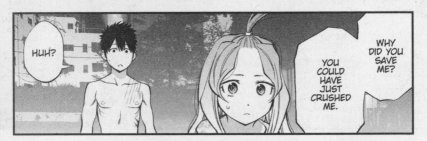

HUH?

WHY DID YOU SAVE ME?

YOU COULD HAVE JUST CRUSHED ME.

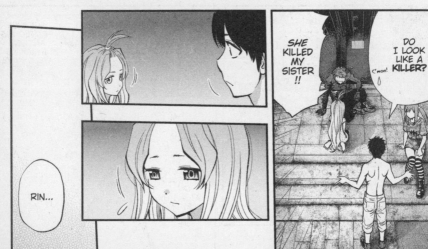

SHE KILLED MY SISTER!!

DO I LOOK LIKE A **KILLER**?

C'mon!

RIN...

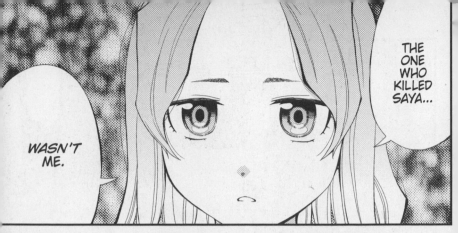

THE ONE WHO KILLED SAYA...

WASN'T ME.

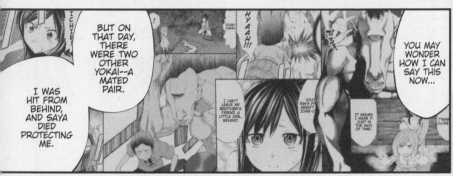

YOU MAY WONDER HOW I CAN SAY THIS NOW...

BUT ON THAT DAY, THERE WERE TWO OTHER YOKAI--A MATED PAIR.

I WAS HIT FROM BEHIND, AND SAYA DIED PROTECTING ME.

ICHIE!

ICHIE-CHAN!

HYAAH!!!

I CAN'T LEAVE MY BROTHER'S FRIEND, A LITTLE GIRL, BEHIND!

YOU'RE RIN'S FRIEND, AREN'T YOU, ICHIE-CHAN?

IT SEEMS I MADE IT JUST IN THE NICK OF TIME!

'TWAS CLOSE.

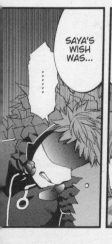

SAYA'S WISH WAS...

· · · · · ·

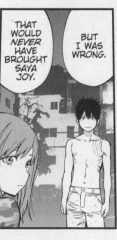

THAT WOULD NEVER HAVE BROUGHT SAYA JOY.

BUT I WAS WRONG.

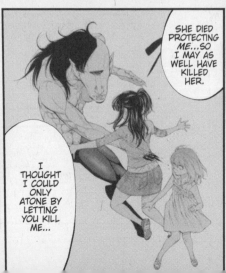

SHE DIED PROTECTING ME...SO I MAY AS WELL HAVE KILLED HER.

I THOUGHT I COULD ONLY ATONE BY LETTING YOU KILL ME...

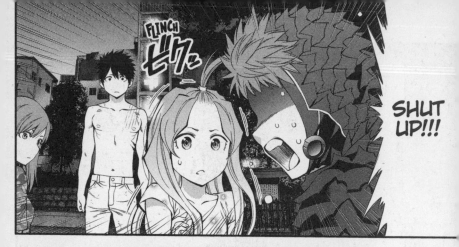

SHUT UP!!!

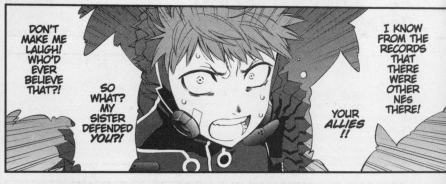

DON'T MAKE ME LAUGH! WHO'D EVER BELIEVE THAT?!

SO WHAT? MY SISTER DEFENDED YOU?!

YOUR ALLIES!!

I KNOW FROM THE RECORDS THAT THERE WERE OTHER NEs THERE!

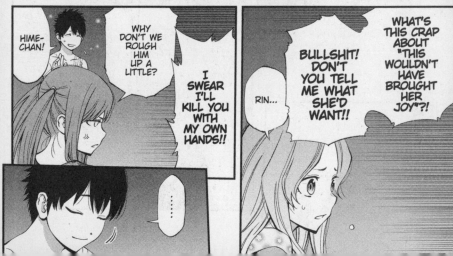

HIME-CHAN!

WHY DON'T WE ROUGH HIM UP A LITTLE?

I SWEAR I'LL KILL YOU WITH MY OWN HANDS!!

RIN...

BULLSHIT! DON'T YOU TELL ME WHAT SHE'D WANT!!

WHAT'S THIS CRAP ABOUT "THIS WOULDN'T HAVE BROUGHT HER JOY"?!

......

SHE'S NOT MAKING IT UP!
WHAT ?!
LAD...
HAIR... ABOUT THIS LONG...
WITH HALF OF IT TIED IN THE BACK... A HALF-PONY TAIL, RIGHT?
CUTE, MIDDLE SCHOOL AGE, WITH SLIGHTLY SLANTED EYES...
IS THAT YOUR SISTER?
HOW THE HELL DO YOU KNOW THAT?!
SHFF
......
SHE'S BEEN HERE ALL THIS TIME...
IT'LL BE OKAY!
DON'T WORRY!

RIGHT BEHIND YOU...
TRYING TO TELL YOU THAT IT'S NOT A LIE!

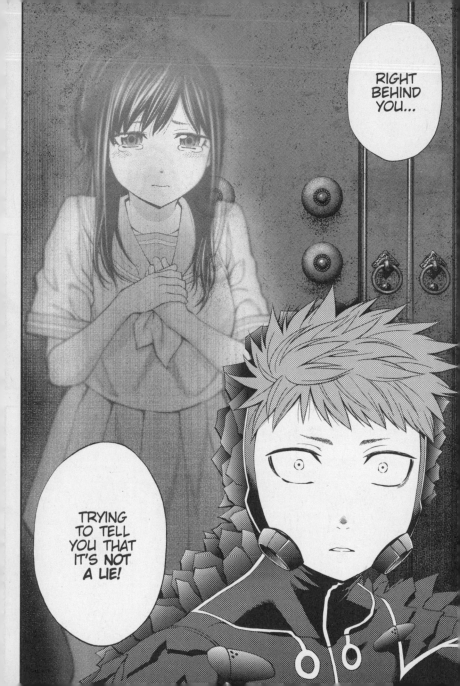

?!
NO WAY!
I CAN'T SEE NOR FEEL ANYTHING!
NO...
AH!
SAYA...
PLIP
SHE IS THERE!
YOU'RE KIDDING ME!
SHE'S A WEAK SPIRIT, THE KIND THAT EVEN SPIRITUAL BEINGS LIKE US CAN'T SEE UNLESS WE FOCUS.

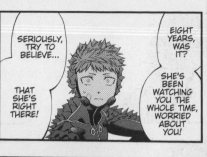

SERIOUSLY, TRY TO BELIEVE...

THAT SHE'S RIGHT THERE!

EIGHT YEARS, WAS IT?

SHE'S BEEN WATCHING YOU THE WHOLE TIME, WORRIED ABOUT YOU!

TRY TO BELIEVE IT!

JUST WHAT ARE YOU?!

YAT-SUKI...

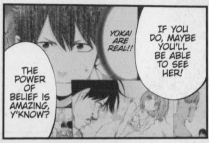

THE POWER OF BELIEF IS AMAZING, Y'KNOW?

YOKAI ARE REAL!!

IF YOU DO, MAYBE YOU'LL BE ABLE TO SEE HER!

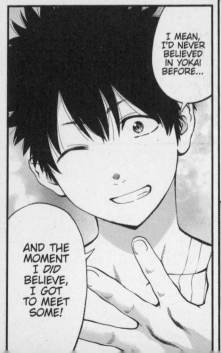

I MEAN, I'D NEVER BELIEVED IN YOKAI BEFORE...

AND THE MOMENT I DID BELIEVE, I GOT TO MEET SOME!

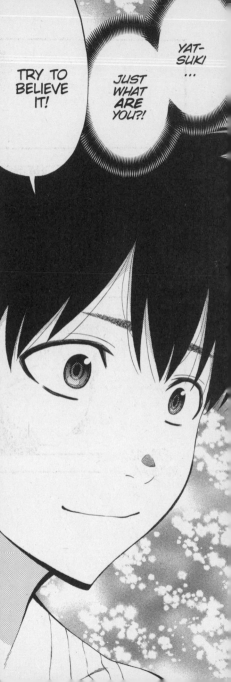

MY
SISTER...

SAYA'S...

ALWAYS
BEEN
BEHIND
ME?

NEECHAN...

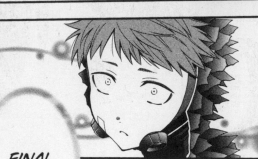

FINAL
WISH...

FOR A
SECOND...

IT WAS
JUST
FOR THE
BRIEFEST
INSTANT,
BUT...

RIN...!
MY SISTER...

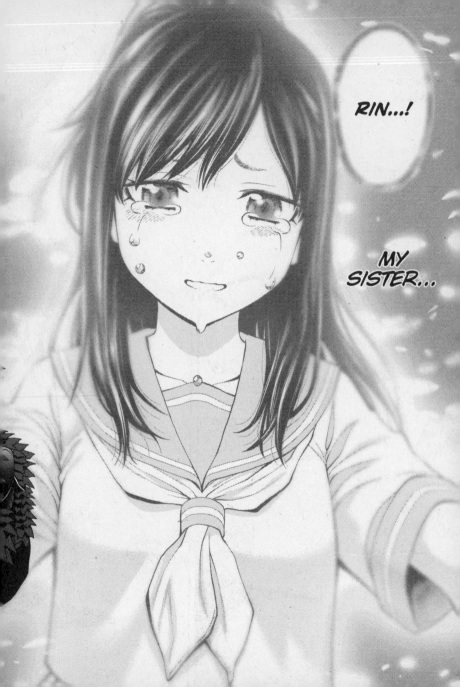

STAY FRIENDS...
WITH ICHIE... FOREVER.
NEE-CHAN...
I KNOW SHE WAS THERE.

WE'RE...

NOT ENEMIES.

BUT WHAT WE REALLY WANT IS THE SAME THING.

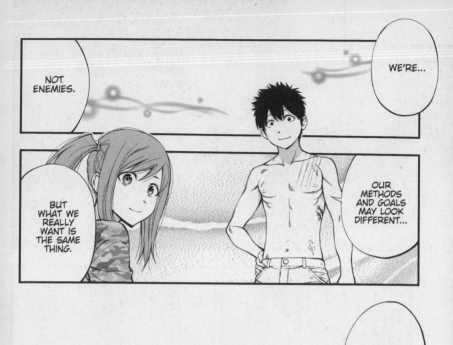

OUR METHODS AND GOALS MAY LOOK DIFFERENT...

THERE'S NO REASON WHY...

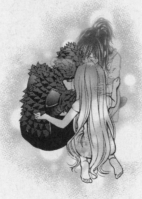

WE SHOULD BE TRYING TO KILL EACH OTHER!

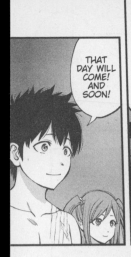

THAT DAY WILL COME! AND SOON!

IF THEY CAN SMILE AND TALK AGAIN SOMEDAY.

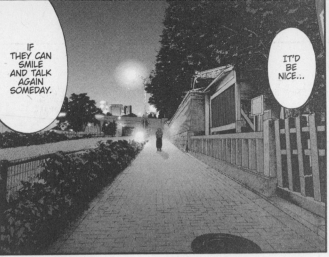

IT'D BE NICE...

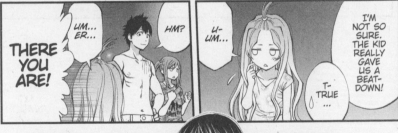

THERE YOU ARE!

UM... ER...

HM?

U-UM...

T-TRUE...

I'M NOT SO SURE. THE KID REALLY GAVE US A BEAT-DOWN!

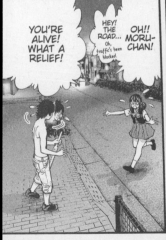

YOU'RE ALIVE! WHAT A RELIEF!

HEY! THE ROAD... Oh, traffic's been blocked!

OH!! MORU-CHAN!

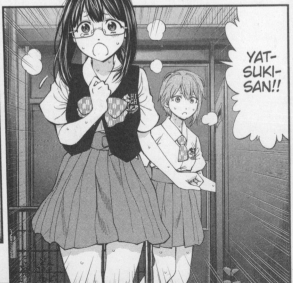

YAT-SUKI-SAN!!

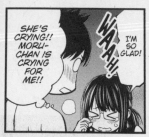

SHE'S CRYING!! MORU-CHAN IS CRYING FOR ME!!

WAAH!

I'M SO GLAD!

HUH?! ALL THIS TIME?! SORRY! I'M TOTALLY ALIVE!

YOU FELL FROM SO HIGH UP, SO I THOUGHT MAYBE YOU'D DIED!

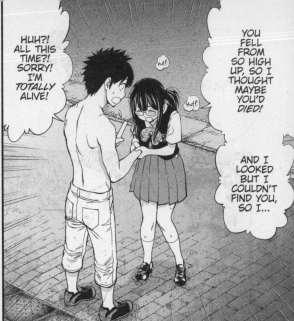

Huff

Huff

Huff

AND I LOOKED BUT I COULDN'T FIND YOU, SO I...

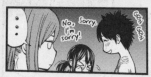

Sorry.

No, I'm sorry!

GON GON

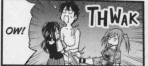

OW!

THWAK

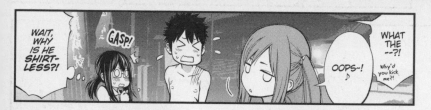

WAIT, WHY IS HE SHIRTLESS?!

GASP!

OOPS~! ♪

WHAT THE --?!

Why'd you kick me?!

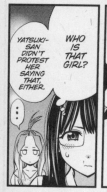

YATSUKI-SAN DIDN'T PROTEST HER SAYING THAT, EITHER.

...

WHO IS THAT GIRL?

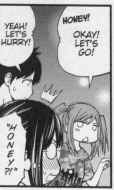

YEAH! LET'S HURRY!

HONEY!

OKAY! LET'S GO!

"HONEY?!"

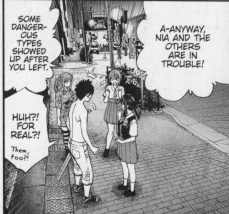

SOME DANGEROUS TYPES SHOWED UP AFTER YOU LEFT.

HUH?! FOR REAL?!

Them, too?!

A-ANYWAY, NIA AND THE OTHERS ARE IN TROUBLE!

THANK YOU...
YATSUKI.
NO PROBLEM!
LET'S GO, ICCHAN!
YES!

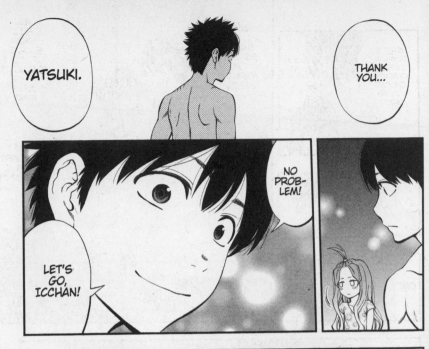

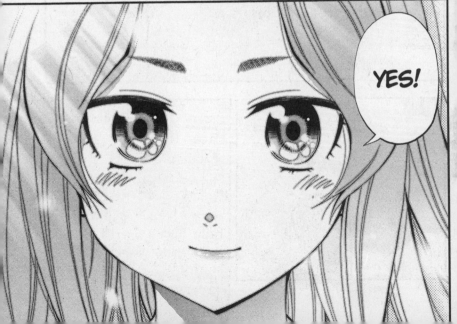

Extra: Icchan and Boots

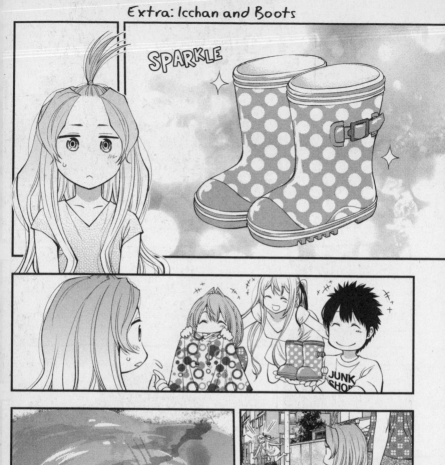

SPARKLE

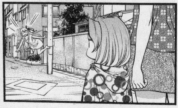

JUNK SHOP

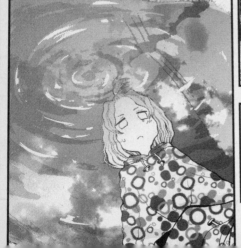

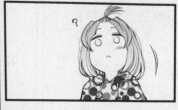

?

JUNK
SHOP

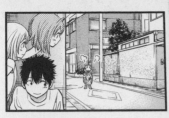

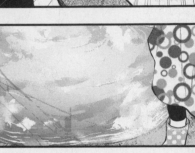

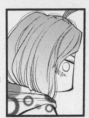

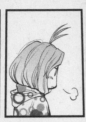

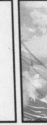

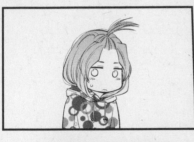

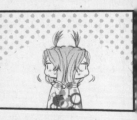

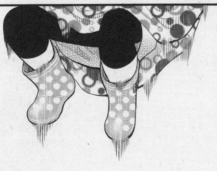

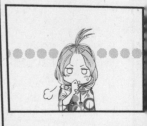

UH...
SO...
SHE... B-BEAT THE HELL OUT OF HOUJOU-SAN.
FOR REAL?
WHAT THE HELL?!
WHAT THE HELL IS THAT WOMAN?!
HMPH!
LOOM
79
Game, Set, Match! ♪

THIS DOESN'T LOOK GOOD!
WAIT! WE STILL HAVE GOTOU-SAN!
OHH!
LOOK! HE'S HOLDING HIS OWN!
BAM
YEAH! GOTOU-SAN IS AN A-CLASS HOUND!
BAM
BA-BAM
TWITCH
FWOO
SPIN
!
BWAAM
......

NGH!
CRACKLE CRACKLE
HE REALLY IS MORE THAN JUST AN F-CLASS YOKAI!
I CAN'T TELL WHERE HIS FEET WILL COME FROM NEXT!
CRACKLE
HMPH!
DON'T TAKE ME FOR JUST ANY PER-SIMMON.
I HAVE LAID TORMENT UPON TORMENT UPON TORMENT ON MY BODY...
THIS THING IS...
HIGHER THAN C-CLASS!!
ALL TO BECOME A SUPER SWEET-ASSED GENTLE-MAN!
THE ULTIMATE TAN-TAN KORORIN-SAMA!!
DO-THWAM
AND HIS RANDOM HIP ATTACK IS OBNOX-IOUS AS HELL!
THA-THUD
BUT...
GRAB
HM?!

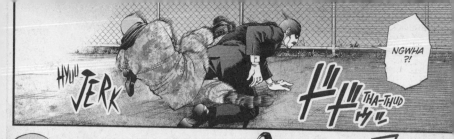

HYUU JERK

ドドッ THA-THUD

NGWHA ?!

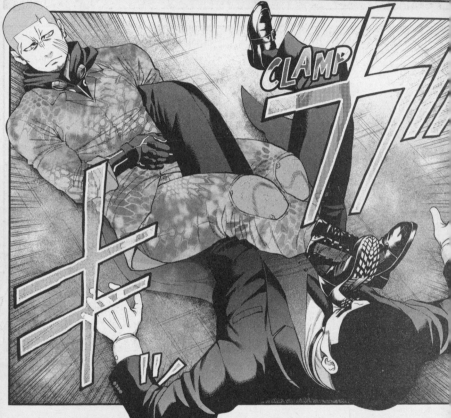

CLAMP

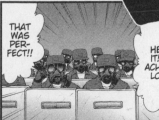

THAT WAS PER-FECT!!

HE DID IT!! AN ACHILLES LOCK!!

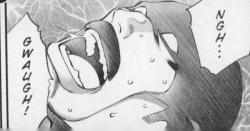

GWAUGH!

NGH...

I'LL BREAK THESE LEGS YOU'RE SO PROUD OF!
HAA... HAA...
CRACK
HEH!
BREAKING MY LEGS WITH AN ACHILLES LOCK? WELL THEN, TAKE THAT LEG...
AND HOLD ONTO IT FOR DEAR LIFE!!
SHRUU
!!

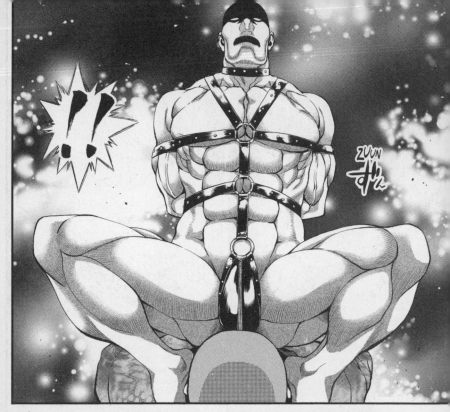

ZUUN

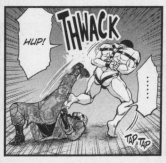

HUP!

THWACK

TAP TAP

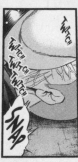

TWITCH

TWITCH TWITCH TWITCH

SNAP

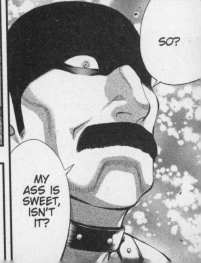

SO?

MY ASS IS SWEET, ISN'T IT?

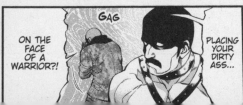

ON THE FACE OF A WARRIOR?!

GAG

PLACING YOUR DIRTY ASS...

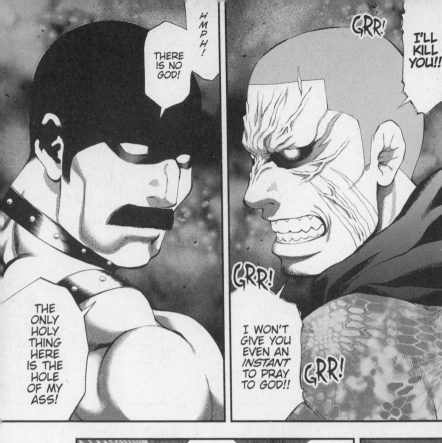

HMPH!

THERE IS NO GOD!

THE ONLY HOLY THING HERE IS THE HOLE OF MY ASS!

GRR!

I'LL KILL YOU!!

GRR!

I WON'T GIVE YOU EVEN AN *INSTANT* TO PRAY TO GOD!!

GRR!

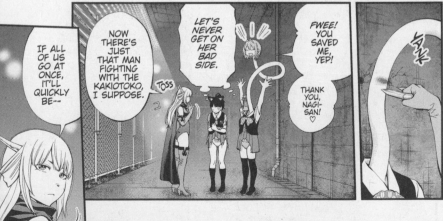

IF ALL OF US GO AT ONCE, IT'LL QUICKLY BE--

NOW THERE'S JUST THAT MAN FIGHTING WITH THE KAKIOTOKO, I SUPPOSE.

TOSS

LET'S NEVER GET ON HER BAD SIDE.

FWEE! YOU SAVED ME, YEP!

THANK YOU, NAGI-SAN! ♡

YANK

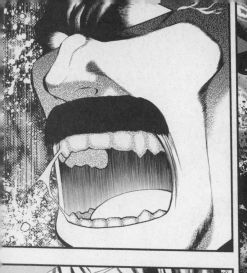

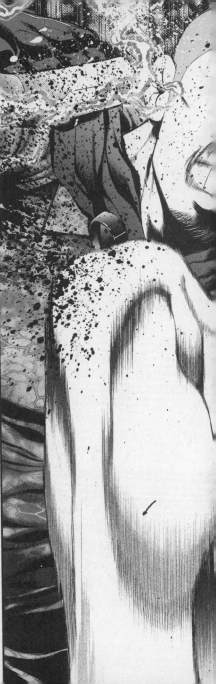

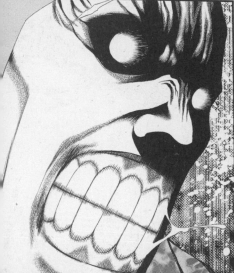

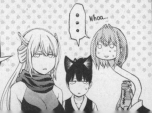

THEY'RE PRETTY INTO IT... BETTER NOT TO GET INVOLVED.

• • • Whoa...

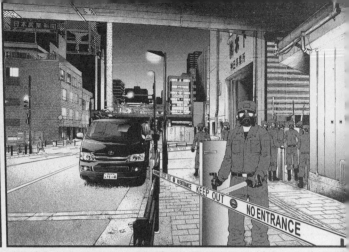

'SCUSE MEEE!

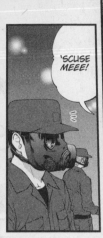

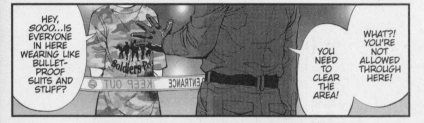

HEY, SOOO...IS EVERYONE IN HERE WEARING LIKE BULLET-PROOF SUITS AND STUFF?

YOU NEED TO CLEAR THE AREA!

WHAT?! YOU'RE NOT ALLOWED THROUGH HERE!

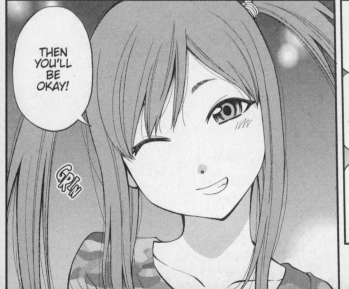

THEN YOU'LL BE OKAY!

GRIN

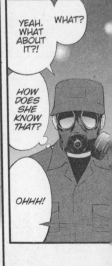

YEAH. WHAT ABOUT IT?!

WHAT?

HOW DOES SHE KNOW THAT?

OHHH!

HUH?
と———ん
WHAM
?!
CRACK
?!
FWUMP
HUH?
GAH!
WHACK
THWACK
URGH!

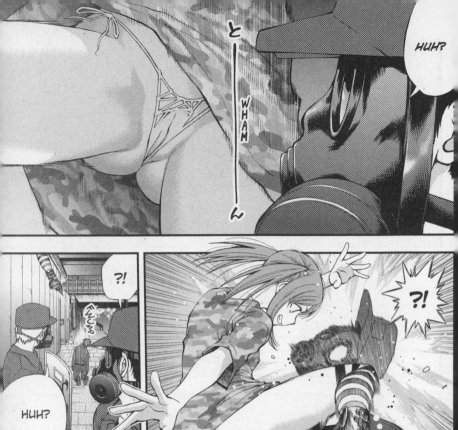

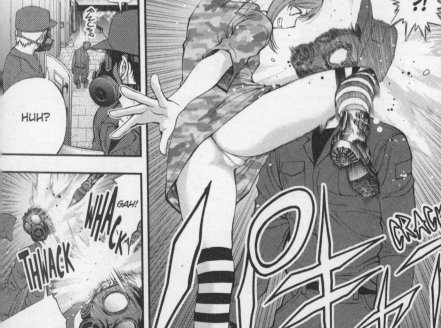

HYUU
?!
WHAT'S GOING ON?!
HYURURU...
THUMP
GEH!
ACK!
DANGLE
WHAT THE HELL IS SHE?!
MURMUR
CATCH HER!
HAVE A NICE FLIGHT! ♪
EIGHT-LEGGED...

CHAOTIC KICK COMBO !!!
GYAH!
BAM
BAM
BAM
BAM
GWAH!
BAM
BAM
YA-HOO! ♪
DAMN! THIS BRAT...
STAGGER
I'LL KILL...
YOU.
GRAB
DASH
HUH?

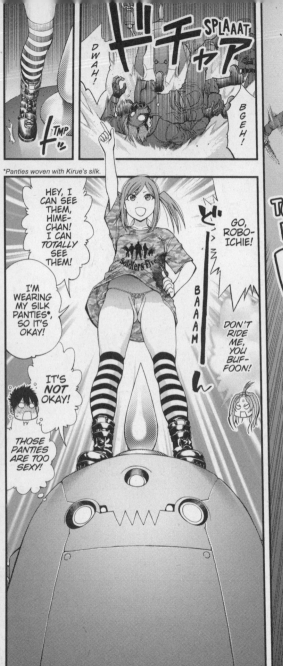

*Panties woven with Kirue's silk.

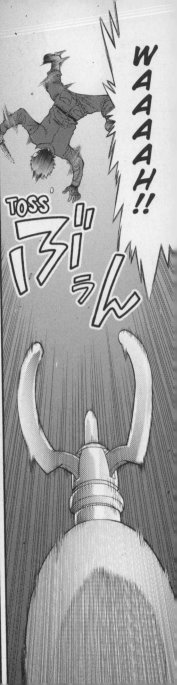

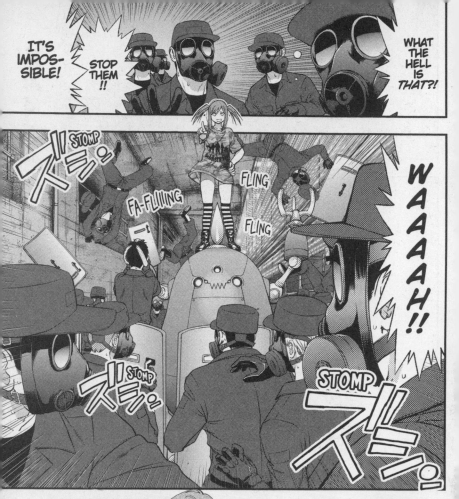

IT'S IMPOS- SIBLE!

STOP THEM !!

WHAT THE HELL IS THAT?!

STOMP

FA-FLIIING

FLING

FLING

WAAAAH!!

STOMP

STOMP

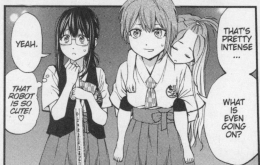

YEAH.

THAT ROBOT IS SO CUTE! ♡

THAT'S PRETTY INTENSE...

WHAT IS EVEN GOING ON?

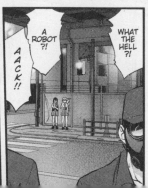

A ROBOT ?!

AACK!!

WHAT THE HELL ?!

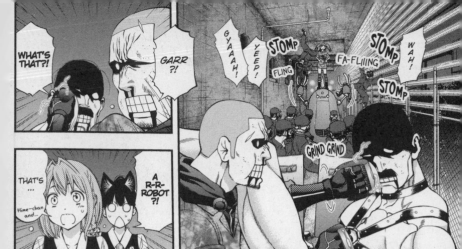

WHAT'S THAT?!

GARR?!

GYAAAH!

YEEP!

STOMP

FLING

FA-FLIIING

STOMP

WAH!

STOMP

GRIND GRIND

THAT'S...

A R-R-ROBOT?!

Hime-chan and...

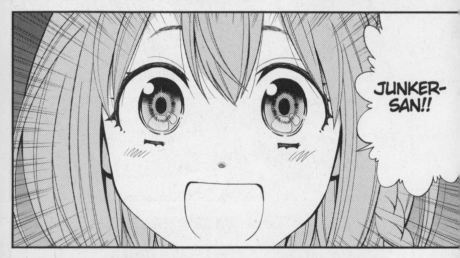

JUNKER-SAN!!

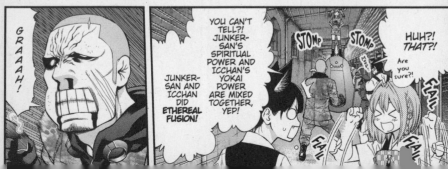

GRAAAH!

YOU CAN'T TELL?! JUNKER-SAN'S SPIRITUAL POWER AND ICCHAN'S YOKAI POWER ARE MIXED TOGETHER, YEP!

JUNKER-SAN AND ICCHAN DID ETHEREAL FUSION!

STOMP

STOMP

HUH?! THAT?!

Are you sure?!

FLAIL

FLAIL

GRAH! GRAH! GRAH! GRAH! GRAH! GRAH!
BA-BAM
BAM
BA-BAM
GRRRAH!!
BA-BAM
BAM
SILENCE...
GRAH ?!
GRAB
GRR ?!
BAM
GRRR!
BAM BAM
GRR...
GRRR!
KICK
FLING
ACK!
THA-THUNK
THUNK

GAH...
......
Hey!♡
TUP
GAME, SET, MATCH!!
You're so cute, Icchan!♡
DU-DUN

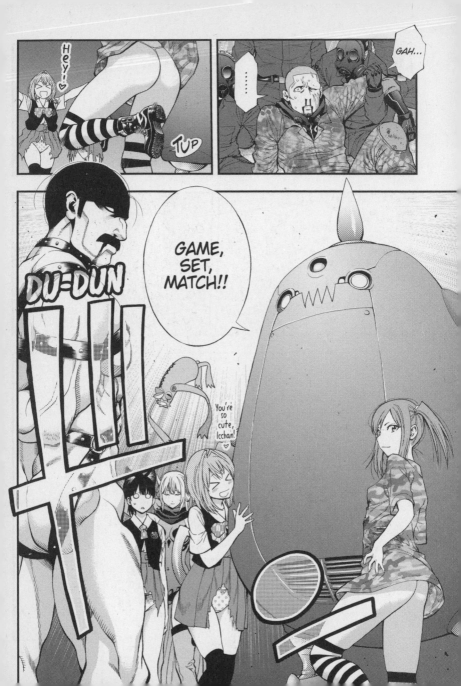

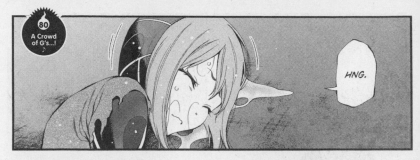

HNG.

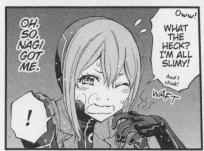

OH, SO, NAGI GOT ME.

!

Oww!

WHAT THE HECK? I'M ALL SLIMY!

And I stink!

WAFT

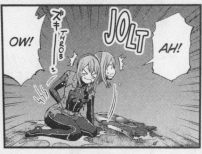

OW!

THROB

JOLT

AH!

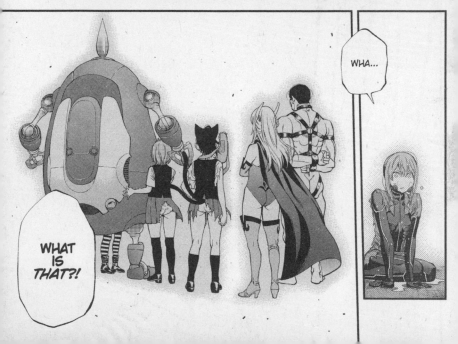

WHA...

WHAT IS THAT?!

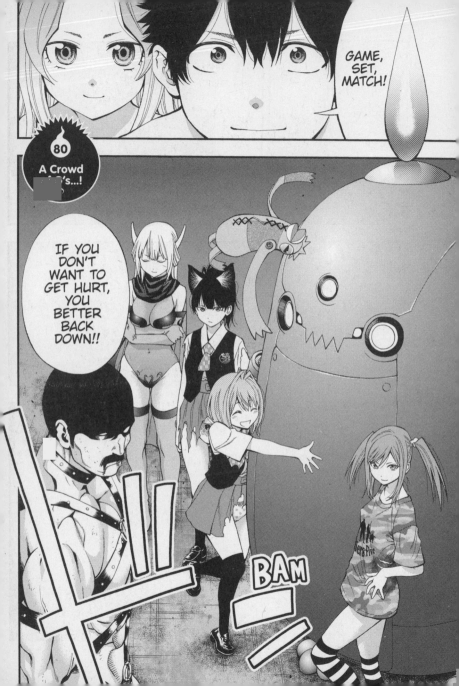

GAME, SET, MATCH!

IF YOU DON'T WANT TO GET HURT, YOU BETTER BACK DOWN!!

BAM

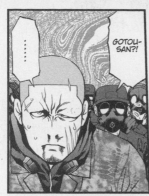

......

GOTOU-SAN?!

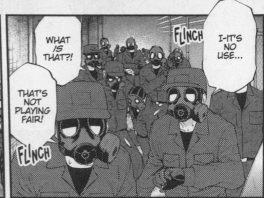

WHAT IS THAT?!

THAT'S NOT PLAYING FAIR!

FLINCH

FLINCH

I-IT'S NO USE...

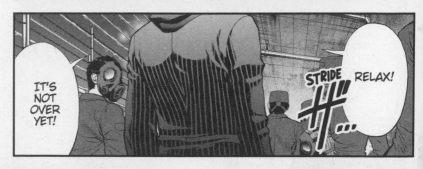

IT'S NOT OVER YET!

STRIDE

RELAX!

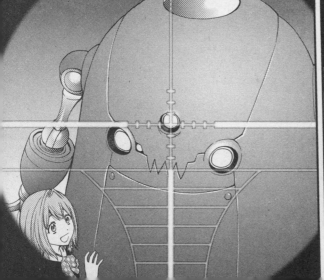

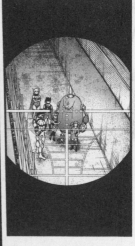

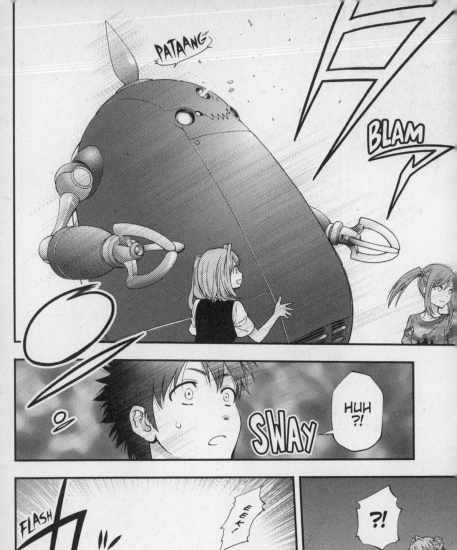

PATAANG

BLAM

SWAY

HUH ?!

FLASH

EEK!

?!

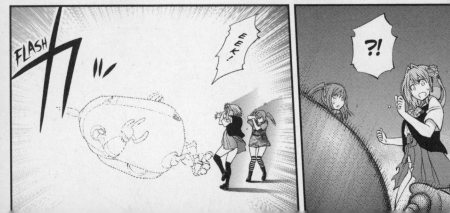

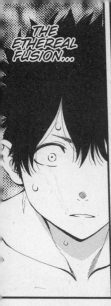

THE ETHEREAL FUSION...

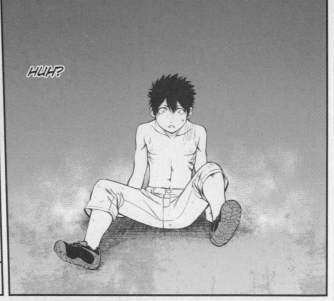

HUH?

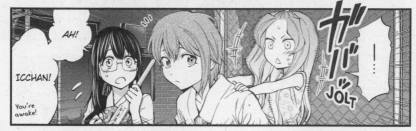

AH!

ICCHAN!

You're awake!

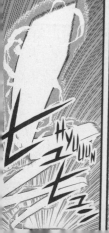

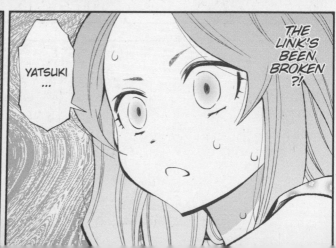

YATSUKI...

THE LINK'S BEEN BROKEN?!

SHYUUUN

JOLT

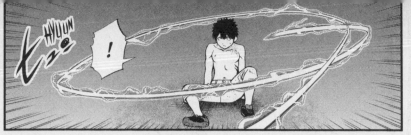

HYUUN
!

WHOA!

GYUU-WSH

THIS
WEAPON
IS...

!

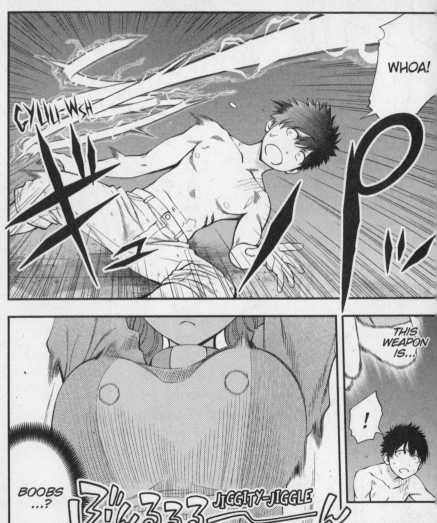

BOOBS
...?

JIGGITY-JIGGLE

JIGGLE
CLAAANG
CRACKLE CRACKLE
KUH!
IT'S HEAVY!!
CRACKLE
SMIRK
STAHL BEIßEN!!! <STEEL BITE!!!>
GAH!
SNAAAP
HIME! JUNKER!
THA-THUD

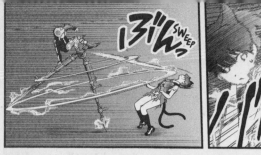

SWEEP

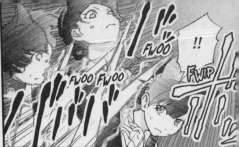

FWOO

FWOO FWOO

FWIP

!!

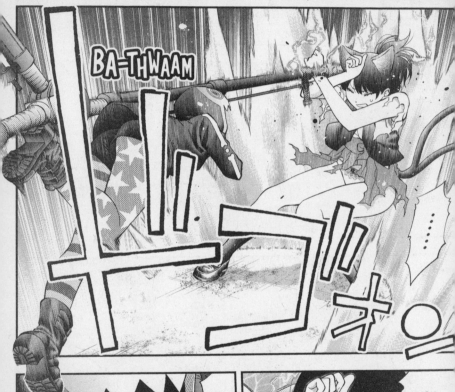

BA-THWAAM

......

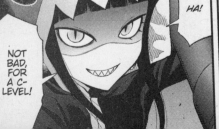

HA!

NOT BAD, FOR A C-LEVEL!

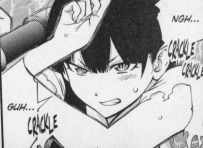

NGH...

CRACKLE
CRACKLE

GUH...

CRACKLE

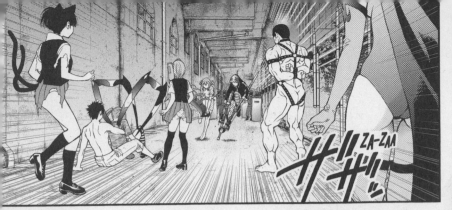

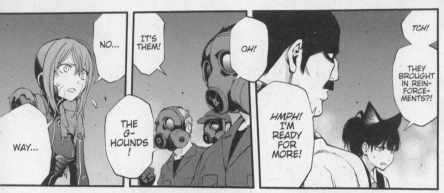

NO...

WAY...

IT'S THEM!

THE G-HOUNDS!

OH!

HMPH! I'M READY FOR MORE!

TCH!

THEY BROUGHT IN REIN-FORCE-MENTS?!

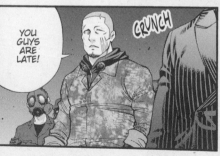

YOU GUYS ARE LATE!

CRUNCH

WE WERE HELD UP IN TRAFFIC, SINCE THE ROAD WAS CLOSED.

I APOLO-GIZE.

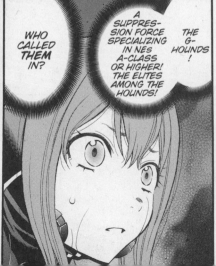

WHO CALLED THEM IN?

A SUPPRES-SION FORCE SPECIALIZING IN NES A-CLASS OR HIGHER! THE ELITES AMONG THE HOUNDS!

THE G-HOUNDS!

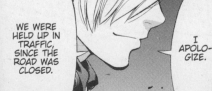

BAM
TRAFFIC? COME ON!
JUST RUN!
G-Hound (A level) **Gotou Ryuuji**
OH, MY! WHAT HAPPENED? YOU LOOK EVEN MORE HANDSOME THAN USUAL!
With your face all puffed up!
SHUT UP!
G-Hound (A level) **Yukimura Junsei**

AREN'T YOUR BOOBS GETTING IN THE WAY?
G-Hound (A level) **Sagara Moko** (nickname MOCO)
125 M
JEEZ! I'VE TOLD YOU, IT'S FINE!
ACTUALLY, THEY KINDA ARE.
G-Hound (A level) **Kiritani Ai** (nickname: Gigatits)
YOU DID IT! A HIT! YOU'RE AMAZING AS EVER!
G-Hound (S level) **Denpouya Yuki**
YEAH...

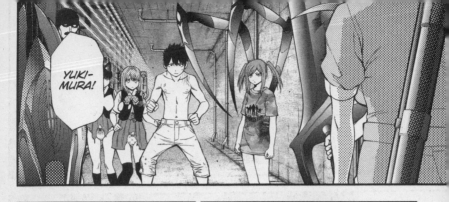

YUKI-MURA!

PANYA!

ROKKA!

ARE ALL THESE GUYS AS GOOD AS YUKI-MURA?!

BITE

Arm text: Roku.

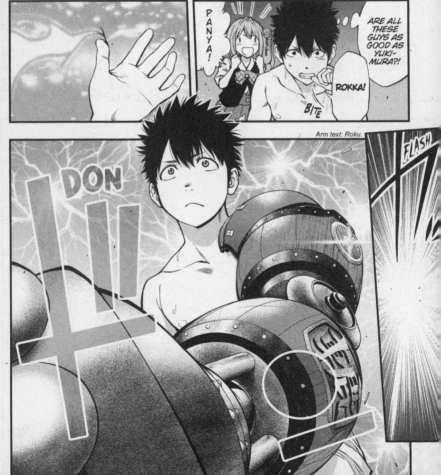

DON!!!

FLASH

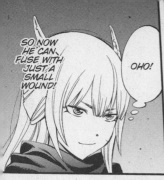

SO, NOW HE CAN FUSE WITH JUST A SMALL WOUND!

OHO!

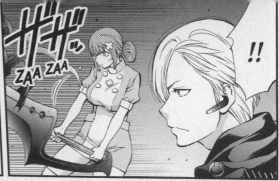

ZAA ZAA

!!

I CAN'T SEE THE ETHEREAL BEAD...

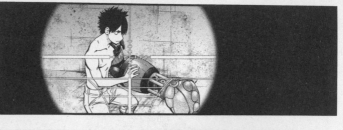

ROGER.

WAIT!

SHFF

MURMUR

I CAN'T TARGET HIM FROM THIS ANGLE.

YUKIMURA-SAN, MAKE HIM TURN AROUND.

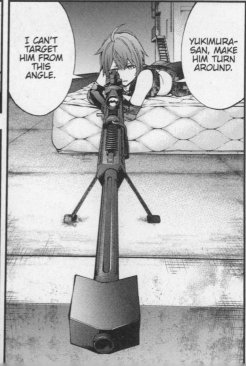

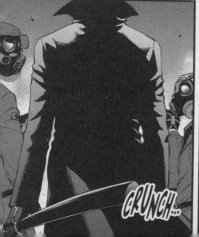

CRUNCH...

ZWOO...

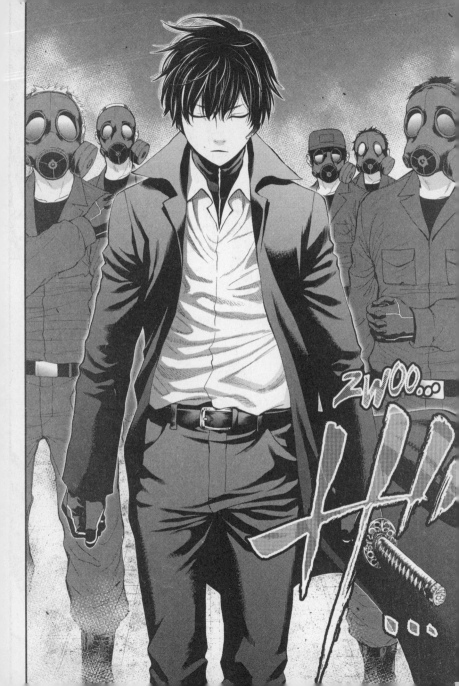

G-Hound (SS level)
Leader
Araya Yuugo
IT'S ARAYA-SAN!
ARAYA-SAN!
THE STRONGEST OF THEM ALL!
THE LEADER OF G-HOUND!
NO WAY!
EVEN ARAYA-KUN?!
ARAYA!
SORRY I'M LATE.
YOU WERE IN TRAFFIC, TOO?
NO, I SLEPT IN.

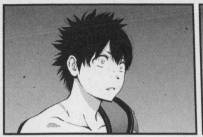

CRUNCH

Grrr!

Slept in?! Why, you...!

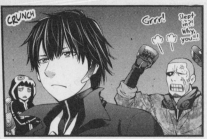

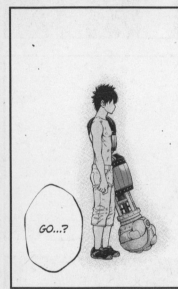

GO...?

YUU...

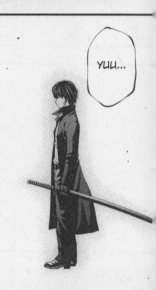

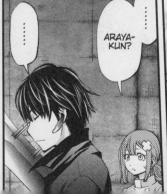

......

ARAYA-KUN?

JUNKER-SAN?

HE'S REALLY STUNNED.

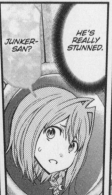

JUNK-ER?

HUH?! YOU KNOW HIM, HONEY?!

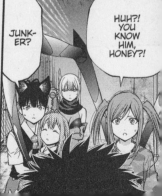

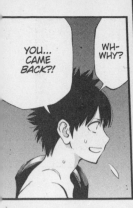

YOU... CAME BACK?!

WH- WHY?

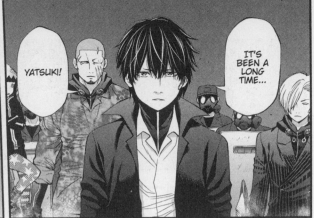

YATSUKI!

IT'S BEEN A LONG TIME...

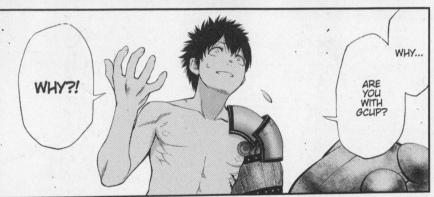

WHY?!

WHY...

ARE YOU WITH GCUP?

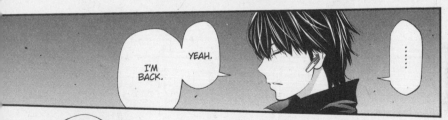

I'M BACK.

YEAH.

......

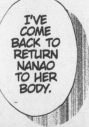

I'VE COME BACK TO RETURN NANAO TO HER BODY.

AND TO KILL YOU!
!!
Yokai Girls 8 End

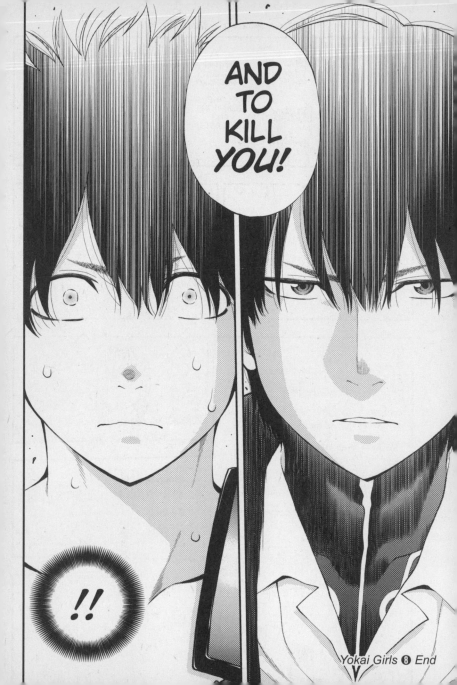

Extra manga: Special Plan 2

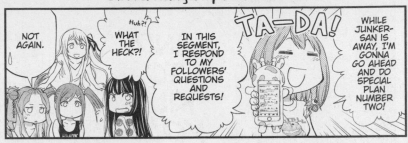

NOT AGAIN.

WHAT THE HECK?!

Huh?!

IN THIS SEGMENT, I RESPOND TO MY FOLLOWERS' QUESTIONS AND REQUESTS!

TA-DA!

WHILE JUNKER-SAN IS AWAY, I'M GONNA GO AHEAD AND DO SPECIAL PLAN NUMBER TWO!

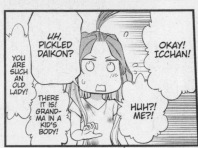

YOU ARE SUCH AN OLD LADY!

UH, PICKLED DAIKON?

THERE IT IS! GRANDMA IN A KID'S BODY!

OKAY! ICCHAN!

HUH?! ME?!

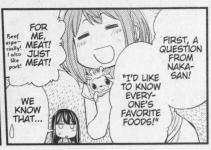

Beef especially! I also like pork!

FOR ME, MEAT! JUST MEAT!

WE KNOW THAT...

"I'D LIKE TO KNOW EVERY-ONE'S FAVORITE FOODS!"

FIRST, A QUESTION FROM NAKA-SAN!

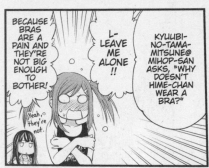

BECAUSE BRAS ARE A PAIN AND THEY'RE NOT BIG ENOUGH TO BOTHER!

L-LEAVE ME ALONE!!

KYUUBI-NO-TAMA-MITSUNE@MIHOP-SAN ASKS, "WHY DOESN'T HIME-CHAN WEAR A BRA?"

Yeah, they're not.

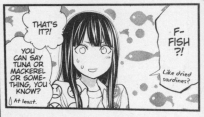

THAT'S IT?! YOU CAN SAY TUNA OR MACKEREL OR SOMETHING, YOU KNOW?

At least.

F-FISH?!

Like dried sardines?

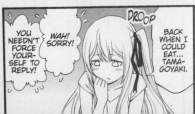

SO, BROTH?! JUST BROTH?!

THAT'S SCARY!!

But cute!!

MEAT JUICES!!

I suck 'em right up!

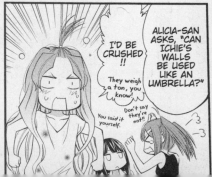

I'D BE CRUSHED!!

They weigh a ton, you know!

You said it yourself.

ALICIA-SAN ASKS, "CAN ICHIE'S WALLS BE USED LIKE AN UMBRELLA?"

Don't say they're not!!

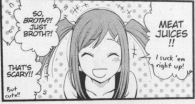

YOU NEEDN'T FORCE YOUR-SELF TO REPLY!

WAH! SORRY!

DROOP

BACK WHEN I COULD EAT... TAMA-GOYAKI.

NEXT, FROM FANIPANI-SAN! "EVERYONE PICK OUT AN OUTFIT FOR NIA-CHAN!"
HUH ?!
WHAT THE HECK?! WHY ME?!
Why? You're asking why?
URK!
C-COME ON! WHAT'S WITH THIS OUTFIT ?!
And where did you get it?!
FLUFFY PRINCESS-STYLE FASHION! ♡
I ALWAYS WANTED TO PUT SOMETHING LIKE THIS ON YOU, NIA-CHAN! ♪
SHE'S NO PRINCESS. MORE OF A STRAY CAT, I'D SAY.
HEY!
Shut up!
IF SHE'S GOING IN A DRESS, WOULDN'T THIS ONE FIT HER BETTER?
H-HEY?! I'M UNDRESSING AGAIN ?!
OHH!
This is cute, too!
I-ISN'T THIS SKIRT KIND OF SHORT ?!
What's going on?!

I THINK SOMETHING A LITTLE MORE BOYISH WOULD SUIT HER.
THIS ISN'T BAD.
OKAY, THEN HOW ABOUT MAKING HER MORE ROCK-ISH?
HMM...
WE COULD GO EVEN MORE PUNK-ISH...
THEN WHY NOT TAKE THE PLUNGE AND DO BONDAGE?
H-HEY!
SOME-THING MORE FETISH-Y MIGHT BE NICE, YEP!
NOT THIS, THAT!
NO, THAT'S NOT IT EITHER.
I'M BACK.
SLIDE
H-HEY... GUYS...
HEY...!
WA AAACK!
ENOUGH!!!
BABOOM

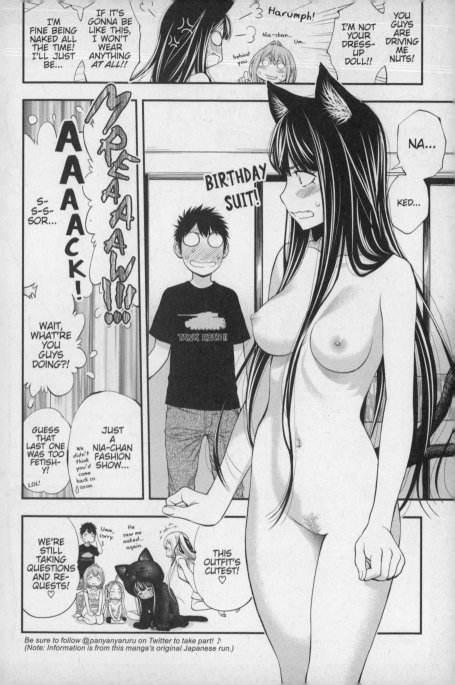

Be sure to follow @panyanyaruru on Twitter to take part! ♪
(Note: Information is from this manga's original Japanese run.)

Yokai Field Guide!

Introducing the yokai Yatsuki has encountered!

UWAN!!!!

UWAN!!

DON !!

SHUDDER
ビリビリ!!
SHUDDER

SHUDDER
SHUDDER

SHUT UP!!!

DON!!!

!!!

BWOO

!!

This yokai appears near old temples. When people pass by, just as it name implies, it cries out *uwan* to startle them, and while they're stunned, it kills them. One theory says that if you yell back at an Uwan, it will run away.

First Appearance: Chapter 76

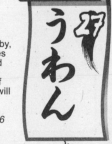

う
わ
ん

UWAN

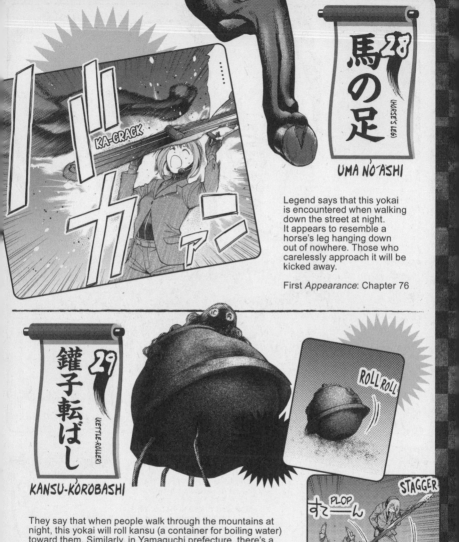

馬の足 28

(HORSE'S LEG)

UMA NO ASHI

KA-CRACK

Legend says that this yokai is encountered when walking down the street at night. It appears to resemble a horse's leg hanging down out of nowhere. Those who carelessly approach it will be kicked away.

First *Appearance*: Chapter 76

鑵子転ばし 29

(KETTLE-ROLLER)

KANSU-KOROBASHI

ROLL ROLL

PLOP STAGGER

STEP

They say that when people walk through the mountains at night, this yokai will roll kansu (a container for boiling water) toward them. Similarly, in Yamaguchi prefecture, there's a yokai called a kansu-koroge, which will roll containers used for warming sake off a cliff toward their targets. They say that if this startles someone into falling, the strength of their legs will wither. Another story says that these rolling objects are not containers, but severed heads.

First *Appearance*: Chapter 76

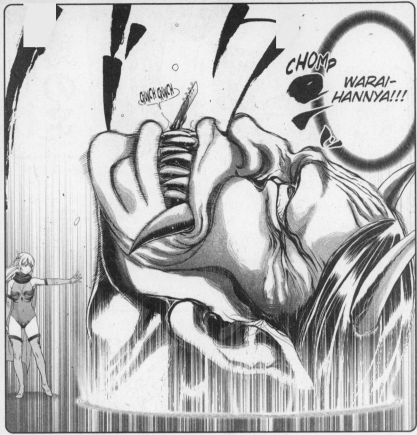

This yokai, a demonic woman with fangs and a face twisted into a mad smile, appears in the folklore of Nagano prefecture. She was originally a normal woman, but hardships forced her to kill her own baby. Rather than leaving it in the wilderness, she decided to eat it herself. This yokai is said to have been born out of that woman's resentment.

First Appearance: Chapter 76

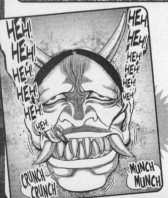

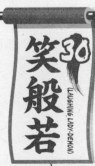

笑般若 30

(LAUGHING LADY-DEMON)

WARAIHANNYA

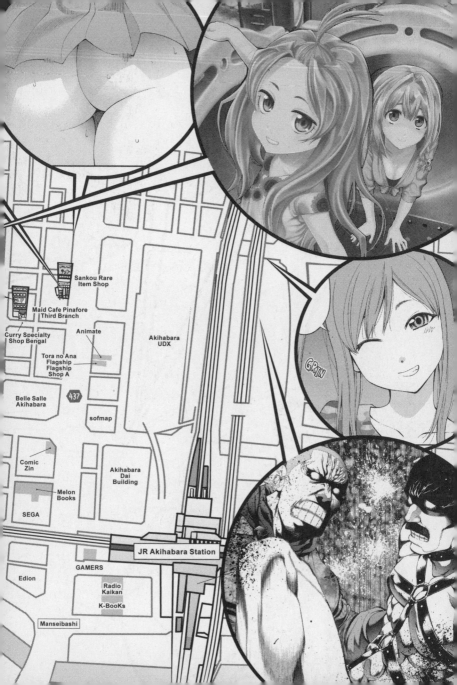

Sankou Rare
Item Shop

Maid Cafe Pinafore
Third Branch

Curry Specialty
Shop Bengal

Animate

Akihabara
UDX

Tora no Ana
Flagship
Flagship
Shop A

Belle Salle
Akihabara

437

sofmap

Comic
Zin

Akihabara
Dai
Building

Melon
Books

SEGA

JR Akihabara Station

GAMERS

Edion

Radio
Kaikan

K-BooKs

Manseibashi

AT THE
ELL IS
AT?!!
ZUZUUUN
Horin
Park
452
17
Yushima
Seidou
YOKAI GIRLS
AKIBA MAP
N
W
E
S
Shohei
Bridge
Kanda River

SEVEN SEAS' GHOST SHIP PRESENTS

YOKAI GIRLS

story and art by KAZUKI FUNATSU

VOL. 8

TRANSLATION
Jennifer Ward

ADAPTATION
Bambi Eloriaga-Amago

LETTERING AND LAYOUT
Phil Christie

COVER DESIGN
Nicky Lim

PROOFREADER
Janet Houck
Stephanie Cohen

EDITOR
Shannon Fay

PRODUCTION MANAGER
Lissa Pattillo

MANAGING EDITOR
Julie Davis

EDITOR-IN-CHIEF
Adam Arnold

PUBLISHER
Jason DeAngelis

YOKAI SHOJO-MONSTER GIRL VOL. 8
© 2014 Kazuki Funatsu
All rights reserved.
First published in 2014 by SHUEISHA Inc. Tokyo.
English translation rights arranged by SHUEISHA Inc.
through TOHAN CORPORATION, Tokyo.

No portion of this book may be reproduced or transmitted in any form without
written permission from the copyright holders. This is a work of fiction. Names,
characters, places, and incidents are the products of the author's imagination
or are used fictitiously. Any resemblance to actual events, locales, or persons,
living or dead, is entirely coincidental.

Seven Seas press and purchase enquiries can be sent to Marketing Manager
Lianne Sentar at press@gomanga.com. Information regarding the distribution
and purchase of digital editions is available from Digital Manager CK Russell
at digital@gomanga.com.

Seven Seas, Ghost Ship, and their accompanying logos are trademarks of
Seven Seas Entertainment. All rights reserved.

ISBN: 978-1-947804-37-1

Printed in Canada

First Printing: August 2019

10 9 8 7 6 5 4 3 2 1

FOLLOW US ONLINE: www.ghostshipmanga.com

READING DIRECTIONS

This book reads from *right to left*, Japanese style.
If this is your first time reading manga, you start
reading from the top right panel on each page and
take it from there. If you get lost, just follow the
numbered diagram here. It may seem backwards at
first, but you'll get the hang of it! Have fun!!

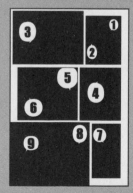